Those people who are interested in obtaining th
and opening their own school of Spanish Mart
contact me via email at:

d1mart@yahoo.es

Previously published titles:

T A U D A N C
SELF DEFENCE AND HEALTH.

T A U D A N C
A U T O D E F E N S A
Y S A L U D.
(In Spanish)

Order this book online at www.trafford.com/08-0080
or email orders@trafford.com

Most Trafford titles are also available at major online book retailers.

Note for Librarians: A cataloguing record for this book is available from Library and Archives Canada at www.collectionscanada.ca/amicus/index-e.html

ISBN: 978-1-4251-6913-8

Trafford PUBLISHING www.trafford.com

North America & international
toll-free: 1 888 232 4444 (USA & Canada)
phone: 250 383 6864 ♦ fax: 250 383 6804 ♦ email: info@trafford.com

The United Kingdom & Europe
phone: +44 (0)1865 722 113 ♦ local rate: 0845 230 9601
facsimile: +44 (0)1865 722 868 ♦ email: info.uk@trafford.com

10 9 8 7 6 5 4 3 2 1

TAUDANC
SPANISH MARTIAL ARTS
Dani
14.03.2005

If at first you don't succeed, try and try again!

Front and Back Cover
By
Dan Giuglea

Dedicated to my family,

To my mother, Maria-Magdalena, my sister Elena, to Ana-Maria Basturea, my grandmother Petra and my father Gheorghe

who has always held high hopes for me with the regret that some of them are no longer among us to celebrate.

To my three childrens and all lovers of martial arts.

To that things which are above understanding ...)

To God who is in everything.
To Spain for inspiring me.

Special thanks to:
REMES, the Worldwide Network of Writers in Spanish for accepting me as a member.

To the European Commission;

Jan Figel, European Commissioner
For : Education, Training, Culture, and Youth, the first person to read my first book.
To Marion Pustkowski, Mary Agathocles.

Pamela Fontainas
Secretary to Head of Culture Unit
Education, Audiovisual and Culture - Executive Agency Belgium.

Ministry of Culture ,

Augusto Paramio Nieto Cultural Contact Point Spain.

Directorates –General of Cultural and Communication Cooperation.

To Trafford Publishing Canada for existing and making all of this possible.
To Alfaz del Pi Television.

To, Alicia Keys and "40 Principales" for accompanying me during the writing of this book with enjoyable music.

WARNING !

The author and the editors of this book will under no circumstance accept responsibility for any damages or other injuries that may occur to the reader due to the reading or during the practice of the contents of this book.

Physical or other type of activities, described and demonstrated in this book may be difficult or dangerous for some people, for which reason the reader is advised to consult with their doctor before beginning the activity.

It is advisable that you consult with a doctor especially if you suffer from asthma, heart disease, anxiety or other illnesses in which physical or mental exercise has not been recommended.

CONTENTS

AUTHOR'S NOTE

The idea of publishing these books arose after many years of pleasure of studies and rehearsals, following the direct continuation of my ideas, of my creative dreams and work, sometimes exhausting in the search for a technique, a work that really satisfies me to fill the emptiness inside and make it disappear for at least a time.

The sensation of accomplishment on discovering that you have finally found the technique and the result that you were searching for, having dedicated your time to the dream and being able to make it come true, fills me with happiness.
The object of this work is to bring a modest contribution to each person's perception, to add some happiness and surprise to those that contemplate it.
Far from being one of the world's great secrets hidden up in a mountain somewhere and without wishing to become a worldwide recognized Master I wish to show a technique which people deserve and which deserves to be known.
I should also mention that many things born in the east are not understandable in the west or take on a different type of meaning.
Being a book written by a westerner the reader will be easily able to understand the practical applications of the techniques and the theory given that some say that orientals have their own language the same as westerners have their own, those who speak English have their own ways etc.

One thing is certain; the way of thinking is different.
Someone said a long time ago, however, that "we are made of stardust" which leaves us many questions and encourages our minds to roam free and with a little luck discover more about ourselves...

Some people pass from a normal psychic life to a different one, others don't. Our subconscious is responsible for many of our actions, illnesses, or healing, so we should speak to it and control it.

The relationship between life and TAUDANC is that, amongst many other things, they are both contact sports.
This second book is not aimed at those who have studied the first but to all people who are interested in learning new things and want to know how to act before any emergency expected or unexpected aggression take place. The body's capacity of performance, the body's wellbeing and resistance to illness are all closely connected.

In this book there are things you can do and exercises that can help you to reduce the degree of tiredness caused by work, enabling you to enjoy your free time and your life more.
Never the less, it is recommended that you avoid overdoing it.

In each technique we will find the relationship between PSCYHIC-MENTAL LOAD, STRENGTH, ENERGY SAVING which should be taken into account so that it can be practised at any reasonable age, building up the work of the muscle groups so as not to lose muscle substance.

Set precautions must be taken to maintain the balance between making the effort and how much effort each person is capable of. Performance ability is very important although it can be trained if it is lacking in such things as: musculature, blood circulation, nerves, tension and other elements.

If any of these factors are not working properly, performance, which is necessary for everything that the body uses, will diminish.

The greater the elasticity of the tissue, greater will be the mobility.

I am only attempting to give some alternatives of an anatomical and physiological nature, to show ways of training TAUDANC style that, apart from self defence, tries to be of help to the reader by demonstrating how to maintain and increase the capacity of physical performance.

In this advanced course of TAUDANC before beginning to explain the art I want to show you how to reason, because it is only possible to practice TAUDANC efficiently if we use this powerful asset that each man possesses, the brain. At the same time, I have to show it the best way I can so that the student with no great knowledge is able to clearly understand the principles. Also so that he can later adapt them if he is in an argumentative situation, one that may arise without apparent reason, or just simply because he wants to practise the techniques for health.

The practical form has been created to be applied not only as a beginner's rudimentary technique but also for the most subtle technique strategies. It can be called "intellectual sport".

TAUDANC is entirely a game of skill and knowledge.

The purpose of this book and the previous one is to develop this skill, whether the reader is a beginner or advanced.

I believe that I have created the most practical and complete bibliography of the art, in the Spanish language, that exists, I have put all my determination and experience of more than 26 years, and others of study and exchanging experiences, into it and I hope that one day Spain will have its own martial arts.

In the first book we spoke in the same chapter of changes in modern day society, well, since then and up until now nothing much has changed.

That is, each day there are more people who wish to have better control of their lives or turn them around, live another way, more in the present, making more out of life, living better and healthily.

If at the same time they learn new concepts that can improve their lives along with the TAUDANC techniques, even better.

In this second book we are going to enter into details getting closer to TAUDANC itself. We are going to introduce its philosophy, its concepts, its techniques which directly correspond to this next advanced grade, entering into the second phase of learning about TAUDANC as a discipline, as an art, as a way of thinking and behavior. It is a superior phase in relation to the first book which was an introduction to TAUDANC. It is logical that the behavior and the thinking will be advanced. A superior grade of consciousness will be practised that will later be put into practice with the purpose of taking the spirit to a higher level of knowledge, of understanding of the techniques, of their goals. To try and understand the relationship better between:

TAUDANC - LIFE - THOUGHTS - CONTROL – IMPROVEMENTS.

I suggest that before you begin to read this second book you stop a moment and think hard about the positive changes that the first book has brought to you as a person, as a student. Meditate on its aspects, its recommendations and arrive at a clear conclusion.

With this clear conclusion in mind we will understand the second phase of the training period better. What I mean by this is that to have a house that will last it first needs to have good foundations and only then the walls, the windows, the front door and the rooms.

The base must be thoroughly understood and applied as a reflex action without thinking. It must already be part of you.

In the present volume you will find many new subjects of great importance. You will become aware of the idea of rejecting the analytical system in some situations and adopting deduction, by confronting the actual, logical and real truth. Adapt to it and treat it as such, the student being part of the system. Skills will be more pronounced the more they are practised and perfected.

Mentally visualizing the study of deficiencies and their transformation into moving targets will help us to get used to real defense or combat situations because a deficiency, as a rule, however insignificant, turns into something pronounced and then transforms into a weak point.

There are many tactical maneuvers that are used in TAUDANC and what they are composed of is determined by the situation and the student. Therefore we have tactical manouvers, trick ones, ones of withdrawal, of making the opponent lose concentration, of distraction, change of attitude from serious to smiling, from a steady look into the eyes to a controlled look to the floor etc. It is worth mentioning the dangers of routine: over confidence, lack of concentration, feeling low, dwindling of desire and energy. The great writer M.E. said in one of his books that "the elite of yoga are in the peaks of the Himalayas." With respect to this I have always felt that the best ones are living

somewhere remote from the rest of the world, dedicating their whole lives to the study of how to possess the powers that are usually called supernatural.

I have seen so many good films, as well as many good masters of martial arts, but I have always had the impression that, in a film, however good it is, everything is controlled by the director, by the group of shareholders, or by the material contributors to the film under discussion unlike those who live in the mountains, that have never agreed to make a film. The reason for not agreeing could be the same reason that E.I.N gave when he was asked to explain the experiment called Philadelphia in which a warship with crew aboard disappeared from Puerto in 1944 and reappeared 40 years later with two survivors. Well, E.I.N said that the human mind was not prepared to receive their explanations about what had happened and he was the first person to say that we only use, at the most, 15% of our brain, and this was a long time ago.

What has this got to do with the book?

Well at any given time in life it is possible that some of us discover that everything is related, all things and happenings are related and that nothing happens without a reason.

TTY also said to N that when he gets out of the car he already knows the street and knows where it ends, if he stays he will learn new things, and the answer to his question was: "But can this be true?"

With this book I hope to offer answers to many of your questions.

I hope that TAUDANC can be the solution to many problems such as health or the emptying of thoughts.

Let's go on to the following chapter.

1. INTRODUCTION

History seems to repeat itself or it is simply the logical path of human progress in all its aspects. I find this is justified with thousands of precedents. So, referring directly to martial arts, with each day that passes they are changing, progressing and becoming an art which tries to harmonize life and health and because of this they can only bring a good and healthy way of living and suitable behavior to our times.

TAUDANC itself is also progressing, and with the passage of time and the new books that will follow we will learn new applications of the techniques and ways of thinking of TAUDANC in real life.
By referring to harmony, we are automatically talking about complicity. Complicity of more or less implication in life, consisting of the goals that each one of us has to have in life.
An obligatory complicity wished for or not, that marks the:
WHAT I WANT- WHAT I CAN - PRESENT SITUATION - ANALASYS OF REAL POSSIBILITIES AND/OR CONVERGENCE to what we have already found since the first time we saw it.
ADAPTATION. Adaptability is very important because many times in life we find ourselves in unusual situations in which we have to find a solution; the same in TAUDANC new techniques arise to solve situations.
It is said that everything is invented, there is nothing new.
Nothing truer, but it is a little ambiguous and at times uncertain.
It's enough to see scientific or other types of advances even in the progress of third world countries. Furthermore man by nature is inventive and progressive, although we all know that each progress has an end. We are born, we develop while growing, maturing until we die, passing to another dimension or passing to whatever each one believes.
The book offers those readers who are interested and the student a very open range aimed towards mental and physical benefits such as self defence. Many applications will be found apart from exercises of self defence and health. TAUDANC techniques combine applications of self defence as a martial art with their specific actions focused on health.
By practising TAUDANC and improving it, every day we are trying to add a healing attribute of many aspects to the style.
We are trying to increase and fortify our interior strength while the spirit discovers new aspects of behavior and reaction.
TAUDANC helps to liberate accumulated tension at the end of the day.
In the second phase of the learning process, which is the first superior phase of TAUDANC, we are going to see how our thoughts, logic and all the rest of components together with breathing, meditation and

performance will rise into an intellectual and practical category. Various positive changes will be noticed in all that is written and shown in continuation.
The techniques are superior techniques of the first phase which means more attention, lightness and certainty in the performance.
A good mental attitude acquired from the first book, and the actions which correspond to the part of you which is called TAUDANC will help you. The technique performances are more sophisticated and more efficient and try to show techniques, at various levels, applied in different ways and combinations. It is not only about movements but also about studying and controlling the opponent's behavior.
The permanent attentive following of your opponent, trying to make him behave how you want him to without touching him, bringing him to the distance which suits you, letting him only get as far as you want him to with his performance. From this point on it is just a child's game. We must not forget the unbreakable relationship between the techniques and the first advanced phase, presented in the first book.
But, there is something that I wish to mention: gunpowder has left the sword, the bow and arrow, the fist and the foot behind.

What if the aggressor is armed?

An armed attack must be seen as a hand attack with a dangerous extension for which the victim, threatened with defending greater power, must be cold blooded and calm. To be able to do this, constant practice is required. Cold bloodedness is not acquired easily but it may be substituted by calmness, preparing oneself mentally for the situation and evaluation of risks and possibilities, keeping absolutely calm.

At the same time, if the situation is not to your advantage, you should stop and try to confront the aggressor at another time.
I advise you not to try and fight with another person who is armed whether it is with a penknife or a gun.
Everything is learnt through trial and error before dealing with real situations without differentiating the student's level of initiation.
The student passes through different levels of TAUDANC preparation as written in the first and this present book.

Being your own spiritual guide, only those that reach the end of the path, which is the complete learning process of TAUDANC, will be able to practise and be capable of applying certain advanced techniques.

By this I do not mean that the person who learns it best can then pass on to the study of the mystical or study its techniques.
But, a great desire without the suitable learning process makes the student commit one mistake after another and the creation of unreal and unacceptable situations.

Lack of practice of what you have learnt puts the student in a

situation of believing that it is enough to be intuitive, not paying attention or evaluating his opponent, which is a serious mistake.
Deep understanding, bravery and practice are a good start for the student and the power of concentrating the mind on an object- X- at any time and any place is also essential.
The art of using any action for your benefit is also essential.
Your state of mind must be free of worries, it must be further away from good or bad, and it has to be a mind focused on TAUDANC.
Fear does not exist for the person who is alert and prepared.
Referring to meditation, I can say that: it does not exist for the person who has no knowledge and knowledge does not exist for the student who does not practise.

2. DESCRIPTION

Continuing on from what we have shown in the first book, we can add that TAUDANC tries to be the path towards mental and spiritual progress. It is a path of learning, against violence, using a positive practice of the techniques which are at the same time full of energy, using dynamic movements of the body applying or modifying them according to each technique.

The student is advised to have a positive attitude, to be flexible and spontaneous, trying to achieve the uniting of the mind with the body and the spirit step by step. To be able to gain total control and the best possible results of this first advanced level, TAUDANC recommends the mental study of the imaginary opponent, always practising, if necessary, twice a week during the concentration and focus period.

TAUDANC Master Techniques, is to help the student pass to the next level of preparation which is full of new techniques, new situations and a style of advanced thinking.

There is no-one that can show, know and master all the martial arts but they can know parts of them or a certain style.

Nobody is perfect but it is possible to reach high levels of understanding, getting closer to the continual perfection of the techniques and way of thinking, with the aim of self protection.

We must learn to simplify things which is usually the opposite of the norm. Many times we tend to complicate things by thinking that it is best to just look at parts of the picture, but its not, its best to look at the whole thing. Be simple but deep and observant, paying attention to “cause and effect”.

How can we understand this? Exactly as we understand the attraction between opposites and the rejection of poles of the same sign.

“Seek and you will find”, ask and it will be given. Harmony should exist between you and the opponent and this can be understood properly by studying the Rolling and Throwing techniques which without a good correlation between the opponent’s movements and your own, neither technique can be carried out, resulting in failure.

The types of the TAUDANC breathing techniques are maintained.

The fight of the bull, of the bull fighter, the flamenco dance and the behavior of the Bull- Terrier mark this style.

Each one in its own time, demonstrating gentleness, harshness, mobility, and style and following.

All the techniques which are going to be shown next are special techniques for which intricate footwork is needed given the high character of ability, speed or specific strength that each one has.

We will do a lot of work with techniques that use a small point of impact making the effect strong and fast.
Also we are going to find attack techniques on nervous points/centres or sensitive parts of the body.
Why are they called Master Techniques? Because they are techniques developed to help you to become a Master, your own Master.
Do you remember? Try to win step by step? Well I say it again, it is very important to learn step by step, with patience and effort.
The attraction is already there if you are reading these lines but you must also take into account that some people, even after many years of pratcising martial arts, do not have a sufficiently developed vision.
There have been many examples of students that get confused easily and make mistakes when making their moves.
Maybe it is because of lack of exercise, lack of study of their own moves and those of the opponent, or less focus and less firm decision.
To get confused while practising the techniques is a sign that the technique is not mastered.
The student's behavior can be of three types:
1. Of defence.
2. Of attack.
3. neutral (those of little development and study feel pressurized by the situation which shows lack of experience.)

3. CONCEPT AND PHILOSOPHY

The concept and philosophy of TAUDANC corresponds to a deep way of thinking about the art of combat. Apparently in some oriental countries the theory is studied for five years before passing on to the practice. I feel that this is too much, but it is true that you need to have a good basis of understanding of the concept and philosophy of the art in question. With time, understanding becomes natural and profound. Both elements help to achieve a free, natural, gentle, fluid and controlled performance at the specific time needed.
Simplicity is one of the basic elements of TAUDANC.
Simplicity brings many advantages, saving of energy, efficiency, certainness, quick and suitable decisions.

TAUDANC's concept and philosophy is geared towards the promotion of health, self defence and maintenance of the young and active spirit. Nobody is invincible therefore I recommend that you always have the basic principles of TAUDANC in mind.

The student's attitude must be aimed towards the blend of gentleness, harshness and elegance in the movements and other elements which are components of TAUDANC, applying them depending on each situation. The step from one technique to another assures the harmony and the fluidity of the style, assuring the correct execution of the techniques and of the breathing as a whole and not each one separately.
It may appear complicated but in reality it is very simple, as simple as closing your fist and feeling the muscles of the forearm contracting, making it hard and rigid, followed by the gentle and slow opening of the hand stretching the palm as if to receive a snowflake.
By this I am trying to explain the importance of the transition from hard to gentle, from slow to quick and the application of the two together in some circumstances, directly referring to the Direct Techniques and counter attack techniques. Both ways of performance are equally important and get interwoven with frequency. However they may be applied separately or together, understanding that while one hand makes a gentle block guiding the attacking element that could be the aggressor's hand, our other hand may apply a technique, a blow with 100% strength. Life is full of contradictions, but it stops being like this when you control situations and find corresponding explanations. Just as I said in the previous book, you must win step by step. Having studied the history and the course of martial arts as much as I can, and referring mainly to the defence techniques, the conclusion is very clear. It refers to the strong link that connects all of them together as a practice, a concept and many other basic or common ideas.

I don't propose to contradict styles, teachers, historians, but to offer something new which is at the same time old. Furthermore, it is not possible to give a precise description without the help of pictures which many times speak for themselves. Despite the fact that the ancient masters of the ancient styles are very critical with strange or new arts, I am convinced that not everything has been invented.

We have to reconcile individuality and recognize that the truth about martial arts, is that there are many truths. The river follows its course. TAUDANC shows how to be aware of life without thinking too much about it. There are many things that a book cannot show you but, precisely because of this, it will give you the opportunity of having the pleasure of discovering them for yourself, a multitude of relationships with TAUDANC. People get used to doing what is comfortable, this is what TAUDANC is about, but in another way, it is about obtaining benefits but in a comfortable way.

TAUDANC's concept of saving energy is still existent and will always continue to be present in the ideas applied to the style. At this level concept and philosophy pass to a superior level of understanding and application, they do not disappear, on the contrary they progress, showing your brain new challenges, new knowledge, and most importantly, understanding that the best way of performing is the one which uses least energy, at the same time being 20 times more powerful than any blow or classic kick.

We will go into more detail of the techniques, of the study of the opponent, his behavior, by opponent categories. This at times will be a process of deduction, explanations will not be necessary.

We all know that a street fight is different to a competition.

Some fights have certain rules and respect, and others don't, but in all of this you must not forget that you will always be in a defence situation, you are not the cause of the created situation, the fight.

Each technique has its philosophy of mental learning and how to put it into practice, the performance.

Don't trust the help of others, do what you can alone don't let yourself be distracted even though they may be well intentioned, you are not yet safe. It is very important that once you have finished the confrontation being the winner, than stop and ask yourself:

why and how did I win?

Rewind the film and analyze it step by step.

This will make you aware of your errors or what you can do better, it will establish the degree of difficulty of the action and that of your opponent.

Don't walk away full of joy and happiness, learn by it.

To analyze our possible action, the first thing to do is observe the effects which are produced once the opponent begins to move, observe and study each one of the movements that he is able to do.

There is a difference between what the opponent can do and what he ought to do. With thought and accumulated experience, the student should always reach an advantageous position, even taking into account several principals that with time will be useful to the advanced student, whether we are defending ourselves or we are attacking. Also, if we are dodging, we may adopt an attitude of apparent neutrality, in this case and in others we will soon see where the confrontation is going and what is the logic and the attacker's reaction. It is a mental process of easy assimilation and custom, successive to reasoning. Later, when experience and knowledge are great this accumulation of reasoning will take on the simplicity and rapidness necessary to all TAUDANC techniques.

We must think in the following way: his attack-my response-my new response.

In TAUDANC in a defence situation the elements are ourselves and the opponent, with these two elements we defend ourselves and with the same we attack to be able to win. I know it will seem contradictory what I say, but it is true, think about it and you will understand it.

There is always a difference of values between two people involved in a confrontation, search for it, find it and avoid it.

Look for the weak points, which is where you must attack, not the strong points of your opponent. In the second stage of the combat, however, the strong points will not be so strong.

There are situations in which you have to be on view to attract the opponent, this works like a mobile trap, it attracts. The double: the repetition of a technique over and over again has the purpose of misleading the opponent, not letting him concentrate, you must be like an insistent fly, unnerving, this will annoy your opponent as well as make him lose control of his movements and yours.

There are many examples of position revealed but I think that for the moment it is sufficient to describe just one of the ways of winning, step by step. Both procedures, once applied, show clearly on the one hand your level of preparation and on the other hand show your opponent your superiority, you lead the game, you control it.

The weakness of your opponent must be seen as an actual opportunity, because at the end what we are doing with our techniques is weakening him. Just like the bull fighter weakens the bull, little by little, step by step. At the same time you will have to think as if you were playing chess which requires much skill, your pieces being: the bull, the bull fighter, the flamenco dance, the
Bull-Terrier and yourself who is leading and have each part, each movement and each technique available to you.

It is not difficult, we all know how difficult it is to ride a bike for the first time but, once learnt, we never forget how to keep our balance and to go straight, taking bends when necessary.

First and foremost calculate your opponent's reflexes.

4. MOVEMENTS AND STEPS

1. Added step,

2. Jumped step,
3. Jumps:
  - of performing techniques,
  - of blocks, turns,
  - jump in side attack,
  - jump in fist attack.
4. Rotation movements,
5. Jump with rotation.

Many of them will be performed and explained in the Master Foot Techniques chapter.

As a general rule movement of the limbs is slow or quick, short and precise assuring stability and balance.

The waist and the hip play an important part in the movement and performance of each technique, whether it be hand or foot, driving with the necessary strength and flexibility.

The advance, the backward movement, the side steps are subjected to the correct position of the hip. The steps are light and are performed with much lightness and freedom. The movements and the steps must be performed in such a way that they don't allow you to be thrown off balance by a push or be knocked over.

Be natural in your movements, at all times respecting the safe distance between yourself and your opponent.

However, the following factors must always be taken into account:
- keep your balance,
- keep the central line of the body,
- perform and maintain the correct postures without having to make an effort.

The purpose of training is so that the body adapts naturally, not only to the steps or movements, but also to the techniques.

Our hands, hips and feet do not move in one single line for which we must anticipate the movement.

We should learn to maintain stable posture when moving and when waiting.

So as to be easily understood we are always going to take as starting point the combat position or the combat position in waiting, which is a controlled and light position, relaxed but controlled, as the following photographs show.

ESPAÑA
Spanish
Bull

Master Hand Techniques

A. Only 2 Examples,

B. Open arms techniques,

C. Lock techniques,

D. Immobilization techniques by strangulation,

E. Elastic hand technique,

F. Trick techniques,

G. Immobilization techniques in grab situations.

5. MASTER HAND TECHNIQUES

A. Only two examples.

Before beginning, remember:

- Your face can have many different expressions which are clear indicators.
- Your heart and lungs are protected inside the chest.
- Your arms are flexed by the elbows and by the shoulders to be able to move in all directions.
- Your abdomen converts food into energy and at times acts as a shield.
- The legs hold up the body and allow you to walk, run, and jump.
- The feet assure your balance.
- Your eyes inspire your opponent.
- The skeleton consists of 206 bones.
- The skeleton protects internal organs.
- The skull has 22 bones which means it is not a whole and can be attacked by parts, just the jaw is a good example.
- The bones are joined at the joints.
- Different joints allow different types of movements, others don't.
- In every movement that you make the muscles are used.
- Muscles contract when the brain orders them to.
- The body has 640 muscles.
- Look after your tendons. You´ve got it?, than follow me.

Example Nº 1

In the two photographs, in the first one (the left) the opponent has been allowed to attack until his arm is in extended position, meanwhile, taking advantage of the closeness our arm has been positioned under the attacker's arm taking control of the direction of the blow.
In the 2nd photograph our arm, which was semi bent extends, provoking the movement of the opponent's arm upwards and, as a natural continuation, our fist having the field free, applies the blow to the stomach, chest or face, in this case the ribs. Both actions will be performed as one with the suitable movement of the body in such a way that the impact is strong, if necessary adding a half step towards the opponent.

Example Nº 2

In the photograph, the first movement against an attack by a direct blow towards the face can be seen. Movement of the body towards the left together with the double immobilization of the attacking arm.
The left hand controls the opponent's elbow while the right hand closes the "circle" controlling the advance of the fist and most importantly, taking control of the opponent's wrist. The 3 movements are applied at the same time, a constant observation of the opponent's movements being necessary.

In the 2nd photo above, the second part of the technique is being performed, which consists of the bending of the opponent's wrist, while our left hand makes the opponent's elbow stretch to the maximum. Here both hands maintain the opponent's elbow as well as the opponent' wrist under pressure.

In the 3rd photo the most simple and most important part of the technique is applied: once assured the maintaining of the two locks on the opponent's arm, the next thing is the short movement towards the front with a short push performed with both hands at the same time.

The goal is to correctly perform the technique in question, the three key points described above being the basis, in this way strength is directed and transmitted to the opponent's shoulder to dislocate it.

The three channels of distribution and transmission of strength through the push collide, added to this is a small frontwards movement, making the point of impact clear and small, which means 100% of strength is applied to the shoulder by a rapid and intrepid movement.

In the 3rd photo the opponent is thrown off balance, but this is only a demonstration, in reality I would call it a failed performance because of the way it is being performed. At the time of this technique being performed, what should move is only the opponent's shoulder and not the opponent.

However, even like this we have caused the physical and mental unbalancing of the opponent and we have created a target which is at our total disposition for a time: time that we should make the most of and continue with other techniques without giving him time to recover.

In this way we have demonstrated master techniques that in truth, by using almost no strength, can obtain remarkable results.

Even though they are simple to perform they are very powerful once learnt.

It is very important that, at the moment of attacking the opponent, we situate ourselves on the same side of the blow's direction, consequently we are able to have a solid position to control the attacking element better, the arm.

B. Open Arms Technique

The open arms technique consists in the simultaneous movement of the arms, normally in an opposite direction to one another, and very often both arms in the same direction.

Another characteristic of this marvelous technique is the simultaneous movement of the arms, one performing the block or the diverting of direction while the other arm applies the suitable blow.

There are also situations in which a blow is performed with both hands following the same direction and having the same action.

Each hand has 27 bones, transforming it into the most flexible part of the body and the most important tool for its flexibility.

Together with its 30 muscles and those of the forearm we are going to use it to practise TAUDANC.

The fingers are also important tools, they can strike, and they can apply pressure. Another very important point that I want to mention is the energy generated by the movement of the body itself and in particular we will be referring to the energy that the hands can generate, here we should name some related domains: reflexology, presure point therapy, bio-energetic massages, psychotherapy, radiesthesia, reiki.

It is strange that in martial arts no one has been heard of that is intentionally applying energy from the hands, why? Because I believe that as far as students are concerned they are only interested in the self defence and where the older masters are concerned I don't know how to answer but I can think of two possibilities:

1.Those that do know how to use this power are so well paid for their services in upper classes and closed circles that they do not need to make films to earn a living.

2. The second possibility is that often we are using this energy but in a state of sub consciousness that does not attract our attention.

Those who can and know how to use this energy are said to have a gift, I don't believe it. I believe that they just know the secrets of learning and its applications.

The energy of the human body circulates by two energetic meridians, one positive and the other negative.

The balance of the two is maintained by another energy called by the Japanese "Ki", by the Chinese "Chi" and by Jesus "light".

A set example is by the gesture of instinctively placing our hand on the place where we have a pain, the head, the stomach or elsewhere.

I am not going to go into details but the practice of energisation, that is the recovery of lost energy during the day, can be recuperated just by placing one hand on the sternum and the other on the stomach for one or two minutes.

We should be aware of and believe in this energy when performing hand techniques, especially the techniques in which blows are used without using the hand in the shape of a fist.

The recharging of energy contributes to the improvement of the body's resistance to strength.

It increases the capacity of concentration, improves the memory, increases the capacity of imagination and interaction and eliminates the energetic unbalance. A simple example is to remember that our grandfathers many times before doing an important action, rubbed their palms together. It has since been proved that by doing this exercise you are favouring concentration in the next action that you wish to perform. Therefore the same energy also exists in the hands at the time of applying blows, and because of this, before applying the blow, we are going to direct the concentration of energy to the palms or the fingers.

If it is practised correctly in a short time the difference between a normal blow and one in which the energy aimed to the blow has previously been transferred mentally will be noticed. The question is: Will the reader understand what I understand while I am writing these lines? If you think that you are going to fail it means that you are not totally convinced of what you are doing and neither do you trust your abilities and mental powers to be able to do what you have proposed. By having mental discipline many things can be done that you did not believe you could do.

The mind has to be trained to pass the necessary energy to the hands when needed. The way of thinking plays an essential role because by controlling it can be directed towards revenge and hatred, but it can also be directed towards harmony, good faith, happiness and beauty. In other words if we wish to apply energy to a palm in the performance of a blow, the mind will do it for us. To be able to have better control of this you must remember that the nervous and sensitive system is self destructive, it has a tendency to break down. A break down caused by being sedentary, lack of activity or too much activity if it has been exaggerated.

We have already seen the chain of function that transfers the energy to the palms and fingers. It only leaves it up to us to put into practise with the TAUDANC techniques. The same technique of transferring energy is also used to relieve headaches or other types of pain, just like our grandfathers used to do with a simple massage on the painful spot together with a prayer. That is, they used the transfer of energy at the same time that they asked God for help to repair the damage caused by the "dark side".

BASE POSITION

Open Hands Technique, aimed at blocking the opponent both mentally and physically. At the same time because of the adopted position techniques of attack, block, dodge and thrusts and many more can be performed taking advantage of the closeness with the inert opponent.

Finally the most suitable technique will be adopted, depending on the opponent's attack. The position which is also called "The Bull fighter's defence" is in itself a position prepared for everything that can arise and that is happening while analyzing and studying the opponent and his intentions.

DOUBLE BLOCK

Also called "The sword and cape" represents a block with the right hand moving from down upwards protecting the upper part, while the left hand is simulating a block to a kick attack in the middle/lower part of the body. The movement is contrary to that of the right hand, that is, it moves from up downwards. The two blocks are performed at the same time. The hands are now ready to apply attacks, counter-attacks, ready for any situation that confronts them or that they wish for. Both techniques are applied with or without movement depending on the situation.

The percentage of expelled air in the performance is from 30 to 80% and variable.

The application of the double block technique may mean also that the right hand makes a block while the left hand, at middle level, performs a deviation, or a deviation while approaching the aggressive element and keeping close or stuck to the back or side of the hand which is prepared to apply the following technique in reply to the initiated attack.

It is also used as one of the essential parts of health exercises together with a complete and wide series of other movements or techniques but we will talk about these in later chapters.
The body weight is distributed in such a way that we will always find ourselves in a stable and mobile position. In the performance the movement of weight is distributed 50/50 on both legs which are in a light position with knees flexed. The back is straight in direct relation to strength with the simultaneous movement of the arms at the moment of impact, absorbing between 1-3% of strength received from the opponent.
In this way the arms and the back are one single blocking mechanism.
In performances with a step to the back, the right foot moves to the back without changing the balance formed by the shoulders, arms and back and in total correlation and harmony with the movement of the feet. At the moment of impact we should find ourselves prepared and it should take place before reaching the end or at the exact moment in which both contrary forces crash.
Depending on which technique is going to be followed next, the strength in the blocks may be of greater or lesser importance or simply a diversion. We should keep the hostile element at hand for future use to our benefit, that of self defence.
If we consider that the technique will be applied with a step towards the front, things change, meaning that it is possible to interrupt the course or the start of the attack begun by the opponent by our action, which changes the strategy. The techniques applied will be different from the two situations mentioned before.
It should also be taken into account whether the step that is taken, is going to be taken with the foot forward making a “welcome” or whether it will be carried out with the foot situated to the back which will mean a significant change taking into account the long movement.
Whichever the situation, the most important thing is: stability, the strength well distributed and administered at the moment of impact and, that everything that will be applied at the same time.

The First Ear Cut

The hands open technique applying a block and a blow while a suitable position is taken with step to the back or to the front. If we are already in combat position only the corresponding rotation to the hip and the soles is applied.

The blow is aimed to the throat or to the head. The right hand or forearm diverts the blow thrown by the attacker at the same time that the edge of the left hand applies the blow.
The movement as a whole succeeds in making the hand that is blocking tend to move to the back and side, while the starting position of the hand that strikes comes from an approximate distance of 15cm, the same starting point as the right hand but with another destination and another aim.

Second Ear Cut

Technique of defence and blow, the defence outwards with the edge, palm or right forearm and application of blow to the throat with the left hand, usually with the wrist or forearm.

The movement of the arms makes an extension between themselves at the moment of application. The movement of the arms have as a starting position the base or combat position. Slightly flexed feet assuring easy movement for the next technique that you wish to apply. Weight distributed on feet 50/50.

BULL'S HORN

Applied technique of blow of the palm together with the block performed with the left hand outwards, supposing that it is blocking a kick directed at a middle level which has been deviated. The action may be carried out with or without a step to the front. The three being performed in one single movement.

The blow is usually applied to the forehead, the chin or the nose. At the moment of application of the blow the hip has a burst of strength of short movement. The block is carried out starting from the position with the arm semi bent and is moved with the corresponding rotation. Minimum strength is applied in the block while the blow is carried out with a percentage of strength of between 40 and 60% in accordance with the moving of the arm. The body leans a little to the front as much as is necessary but without losing balance.

BULL" S HORN BLOCK

Double block to the side that usually is applied against kicks or side blows or any type of blow that comes from the side and is performed with much strength.

The performance has as starting point the base or combat position. Action is performed with the movement of the body towards the hostile element which is being used to attack, followed by a slow change of position of the soles to the direction indicated by the movement of the hip, it is more a calculated drag.

Application Of The 2 nd Ear Cut

The application of the technique is carried out with a body movement to the left situating ourselves almost in the same longitudinal line as the opponent's feet. The opening of the arms starts from the same point each one to their destination.

One of the important elements of the performance of this technique is the continuous control carried out by the back of the left hand which is stuck to the opponent's fist or arm, this is a great advantage. By widening more the opening of the arms without moving the left one, we will obtain a stronger blow and the performance will be longer. In the photo the blow is short and quick.

Another Application of The 2 nd Ear Cut

Application of the same technique but from front, without side movement, the blow is following block´s direction. This is a rapid action with the application of a rapid blow without trying to change the opponent's position. However, if you wish to apply more strength to the blow this will throw the adversary off balance. As you have already seen, the position of the right palm is also facing another way and direction.

Application of Bull's Horn Block

Technique carried out with body movement to the left, right foot bent as much as necessary to sustain the body at the moment of impact. To give the block greater power the fists have been used.

Using the fists in the block automatically implicates the use of them in the first techniques that follow which are going to be applied as blows. What has been done in this performance, from the combat or basic position the opponent's blow has been allowed to follow its direction, while in the meantime, we have left the path open taking a closer position and applying the blow. With this advantageous performance and position we have created a free field of action in the application of short range techniques. Do not forget the permanent contact of the left arm in this performance, the right hand must be prepared to follow with a blow or a block against a possible attack by the opponent, pay attention to the left hand.

Open Arms Technique with Application of Blow to the Shoulder

As it can be seen a blow with the edge of the hand on the opponent's shoulder has been applied, it can also be applied to the collarbone, but in this performance what we want is to lock the shoulder. Pay attention to the permanent contact of the right arm. The blow is short and precise.

I thought it would be a good idea to give you at least a continuation of the Open Arms Technique that can be applied.
Here it is. Wrist lock together with elbow lock which may be followed by a blow to the head with the left fist, then the application of the foot cut etc.
The open arms techniques achieve the strength of the application through the so called channels and I refer to the essential parts that contribute with their strength to the performance of these techniques.
The order although it is not the only one can be :
- Starting point, base position, combat position, combat in waiting position.
- The rotation of the hip and the body towards where the technique is going to be applied. This implicates the automatic dragging of the soles and faces them in such a way that corresponds completely to the new position giving a sensation of lightness and comfort whether in a stable position or as in preparation of the following movement.
- The performance of the opening of arms with the three strengths differently distributed. The arm which blocks will have lesser strength than the arm which applies the blow, depending on the situation it may be the other way around. But both will receive a third strength of help which will be generated and transmitted by the hip through the shoulders. Also with the help of the energy generated by the correct breathing, correct expelling of air in the moment of each action, in our case trying to apply a single exhaling which means the performing of all the elements as one, in a single time.
- Control of the blocked arm or foot by continuous contact will be for a necessary time and only when it suits us.
Remember that you always have at your disposition many techniques such as: the Foot Cut, the Butts, and Rolls etc.

C. LOCK TECHNIQUES

The purpose of the Lock Techniques is to make it impossible for the opponent to use the element on which the technique is being applied. Usually locking is considered an excessive stretching of one or more ligaments done by applying strength.
The power corresponding to the size of the element in question, on the upper and lower parts both directed in the same direction and in certain situations in opposite directions but always with the same intention, locking.
Again we have to mention the CONTROL factor, while you are performing a Lock technique you will always have 99% control of your opponent. As you can see, control is in everything, it surrounds us, so pay attention and always control your opponent and his movements, recognize and avoid false movements.
Locks may be applied not only on arms and feet but also on the neck, shoulder etc. The ways of applying them are many as the positions of performing them. A useful technique in short distance combat and applied with much success as a "welcome" technique when the attacking element is getting closer.
Yes, you have understood correctly, is getting closer, because you must move forwards and welcome him with a lock, following the path of his attack or taking an advantageous position with the aim of obtaining the greatest efficiency and stability in the performance.

Elbow and shoulder lock.

Performed by starting from combat position and applied on the arm which was directing the blow to the head.
Simply the right arm has been placed on top of the opponent's arm together with a forward movement which has made the opponent's hand stay on our shoulder, creating the two points of twist. If we wish to increase the technique to 100% we only have to :
- move the left foot back,
- increase the grip on the opponent's shoulder,
- stretch the right arm pushing on the opponent's neck,
- add more pressure on the elbow by resting our right arm on it also, or simply reducing the distance between our arm and waist.
More examples in the following chapter, in chapter G. and others where the techniques are used as a mix.

Foot lock with the action of side step at the same time that the technique is applied. Feet moderately flexed. Weight distribution of 60% on the front foot and 40% on the back one. The body is in a leaning position of 10-15º towards the opponent, subject to increase depending on the opponent's reaction.

Roll lock on the inner part of the elbow.
In defence from an attack the fist has been diverted with the left palm, while the right arm is getting prepared to position itself in the ideal place for the application of the inwards elbow lock.

The lock will be applied by adding a forward movement to be able to take the corresponding position.
The most important thing at this moment is the grabbing of the opponent's fist and its rotation to the left and the correct positioning of the right arm.
The positioning of the right arm is done by a blow of low intensity and strength but by applying enough strength for the opponent's arm to be bent sufficiently for us to be able to position our arm correctly. In the photograph below the correct positioning of the arm is shown and the forced bending is done at the same time as the lock on the opponent's wrist.
The performance also depends on the movement which we must make towards and in front of the opponent, helping the arms maintain and increase the degree of locking, maintaining the control of the arm and of the action.
The right foot gets closer to the opponent by a movement to the front, short and safe taking a stable position.

It is the same attack but the defence by locking will be different. Considering that the attacking hand is in a straight position we grab the opponent's fist again with our left hand and in continuation, the right palm grabs the opponent's elbow.

Once we have applied both grabs we pass to the application of the bending of the opponent's arm by performing a push to the front and downwards action with the left hand, and a gentle but firm pull of the opponent's elbow towards us with the left palm and right arm. The opponent's arm having been immobilized in the present position (photo 1) has a downwards bend of 10-15 degrees, preparatory bend for the application of the following movement described as the second part of the performance.
To apply the second part of the performance the left hand presses and twists the opponent's palm, the right hand grabs the opponent's forearm.

In this instant the real performance of the technique begins by joining together all the necessary elements. The palms which grab the opponent's arm perform a lock by twisting at the moment that the body takes a new position moving backwards.
It is a double lock.

D. IMMOBILIZATION TECHNIQUES BY STRANGULATION

Strangulation techniques, which by their action implicates also a certain immobilization of the opponent, are techniques used not only when standing and are applied many times in combination with other techniques such as locks. It is a short range technique that implies knowledge of the weak points, arteries, breathing channels and other points considered very sensitive with immediate reactions from the opponent, weakening him seriously.
By this we understand that we can put pressure on an artery and partially interrupt the transport of blood towards the brain, like also putting pressure on a internal respiratory track will produce the decrease of expelled air, air that is also needed by the blood for good functioning. I will not go into too many details but I will just say that the arms are the elements used to perform this technique and only in 20% of situations will the feet be used.
Next I am going to present some examples of immobilization by strangulation which can help you understand the importance and the easy use of this technique, so useful especially in short distances.
I say especially because strangulations using the feet are mid and long distance techniques. Let us see four completely different examples, some applied on the same point.

In the previous photo we have the application of strangulation using "ribbon ends", the extremities of the opponent's clothes.
The performance consists in grabbing the outer parts of the neck of the opponent's clothes, the hands situating themselves in a symmetrical position. From here we will begin to apply the strangulation with the simultaneous movement of the fists grabbing the clothes; in our case the left arm pulls to the right while the right arm pushes forward. With the action of both arms moving in opposite directions we have carried out a strangulation of the opponent's neck who in a short time will be without air. Be careful with this technique which can be dangerous if applied without knowing it in detail and its effects. The idea is to control the opponent not to cause him irreparable damage or put his life in danger.
Remember that it is about immobilizing the opponent nothing else.

In the photo below we have another form of immobilization by strangulation where, again, the main performers are the fists that have grabbed the opponent's clothes, but the application is different and the point on which it is applied also. We will begin by grabbing the opponent's clothes hard for a moment during which our arms will be a little bent. From this position we have two possible ways of action:
One, squeezing the respiratory tracks with the thumbs, the fists making an inward rotation at the same time that the little fingers are as far out as possible, closing the "circle" by resting on the clothes in such a way that the diameter of the neck of the clothes is considerably reduced, achieving the performance of the technique. The second possibility is to apply a complete rotation to the fists in the opposite direction to the one applied in the first application, and in this case it will be the little fingers that are going to squeeze helped by the clothes which will act as a support. Depending on the situation the arms stretch out or the extension is reduced in such a way that the strangulation gets stronger.

A good example of strangulation with just one hand.
The "tie" is formed by the grab of the clothes, the pull backwards and down and the application of strength in an opposite direction, performed with the same hand on the shoulder and upwards. At the same time the elbow is carrying out an elbow lock on the opponent.

The left hand is pulling in an opposite direction to the right hand at the same time that it keeps the opponent's hand stuck to the right arm and the body, having total control of movement on the opponent through the arm.
It is used in application of direct blows initiated by the opponent with or without side step, to the right in our case.

The following example uses strangulation through two actions on different points and with a wide effect.
Starting from the combat or base position, we make a circling movement of the opponent to the left. In this movement, with the right hand we grab

the neck of the opponent´s clothes wile we continue moving until we get behind the opponent.
Finding ourselves in this position we apply the strangulation with both hands pushing in opposite directions and stuck to the opponent.

E. The Elastic Hand Technique

The components of the elastic hand technique are:
-positions that may be combat, base (open arms techniques),
-combat in waiting.
The movements of the body at the moment of the application of the blow are to the side, or to the front together with the application of the blow at same time.

The application of the technique consists in performing the components just as one. It is worth mentioning two things:
- The performance of the application of the blow is characterized by the rapid to and fro movement of the arm.
- The arm projects a straight line of strength composed of and transmitted by:
1. the hip, 2. the back, 3. the shoulder, 4. the suitable stretch of the performing arm. It may be performed with side step or to the front usually using the front foot. However in certain situations a movement of both feet may be applied to the front with the aim of reaching the object, face, abdomen, neck. The blows may have various directions which we will see next. In some way it is similar with the performance of WESTERN BOXING techniques, called Boxing in popular terms.
I only say that it is similar but not the same. In TAUDANC the application of this technique involves the elasticity of the arm and the movement together with the necessary rotation of the fist at the moment of impact. On the other hand, in the majority of cases the technique is applied in reply to an attack thrown by the opponent, together with the adoption of the side posture, that is, counterattack from the sides. I will go even further by telling you that just this technique alone uses the attack from the sides in 95% of cases, this being the main characteristic of the performance. The blows have the same path as the blow thrown by the opponent with the difference that the starting point begins a little behind the arm of the opponent.

In the photo, in continuation from the previous photograph the performing of the front blow with short step in front, moving only the front foot forwards.
The impact is done at the moment that the front foot touches the floor.
Left hand in rearguard, body weight distributed by 60% and 40%,

the 60% on the front foot, the soles facing to the left some 10-15 degrees. The hand never extends to the maximum, it is a rapid to and fro action. The application of the blow rises on its way, propelled by the body through the shoulder.

ELASTIC HAND, SIDE BLOW

In the photo below the starting point of the side blow is shown.
It is composed of 3 actions:
1. the preparation of the movement,
2. the movement of the front foot towards the front and side together with 50% of the arm movement in its path towards the target (left hand is poised on guard) and finally,
3. the bending of the body together with the blow application.

Much attention must be paid to lightly following the movement of the body with the soles of the feet, assuring a perfect balance at all times. The components are carried out as one using speed on impact and in the to and fro arm movement.

In the second phase of performance, the body is already on its way towards the final position of the action. The arm which will apply the technique is half way towards the target, moment in which the controlled expulsion of air is applied which takes place at the moment of impact.
Left hand in defence position.

It is a common action with little energy spent and of great impact. The result of the application of the blow, for example to the side part of the opponent's head, will make him move back.This offers us free field of action from an extremely good position and with the advantage that his mind, for the moment, has stopped working, which gives us another advantage, to continue applying other techniques.

ELASTIC HAND, SIDE BLOW 3RD PHASE

In the last of the 3 actions of the performance we can observe the final position of the body, the arm at the end of its journey and the moment of impact. As you can see due to our specific movement we have gone into the opponent's weak point, the side, which in his attack has gone to the front.

If the opponent's blow is of greater power and speed, a corresponding position will be adopted situating the left foot much more to the right and the back, obtaining a more consolidated position and corresponding to the opponent's strength.

The Elastic Hand, Adrenalin Blow

The performance is also from the side although it may be applied straight on with good results. The bending of the body is more accentuated and the body weight distribution reaches 70 and 30%, 70% on the right foot to give stability and force to the blow.

It may be applied to the stomach as well as the chin, from the side, from under the opponent's arm and from a low position, to the testicles. We will have the left hand prepared to give the following blow and the left foot ready to apply a foot cut technique.

Some Practical Examples

Side blow in attack .

Front blow from the side.

Side or front blow in defence. Twist and balance, good stability, good direction of impact in the same direction as the attacker but downwards.

In the Elastic Hand Techniques, elasticity may be applied to the arm by the to and fro movement, by the application of the desired blow with a short permanence time on the point of impact of 1-2 seconds, giving the blow its character of blow, followed by a push generated by the performing arm.
In this performance the technique must be directed in the correct line of transference of strength and energy sent by the line formed by the above factors, getting in line during movement and the forces being perfectly lined up at the moment of impact.
It must be practised before having a real fight or rehearsed with a partner to get used to maintaining the necessary balance at the moment of impact.
All the strength and energy is transmitted by the shoulder through the arm and the fist. The direct front blows that is without side step are very successful being applied at medium level, especially abdomen and sides.
The blows applied with side step have, by definition, the same direction and way as that of the opponent, usually to the front.
Using side step the path of the attackers' blow is avoided but it is very important to study the behavior and the correct position of the body at the moment of application of the blow.
As a supplementary commentary I will mention that the foot which has less body weight always has an immediate use for application of foot cuts techniques, due to its greater and rapid movement, while the other foot takes charge automatically of the body weight for the short time necessary to do the technique.
The other part of the performance which contributes to stability at the moment of the application of the foot cut is the arm that has to grab or push in the opposite direction of the cut.
It is its responsibility to coordinate the relationship of strength in such a way that the body which is still moving will always have the correct and necessary stability.
Talking of steps to the front, in performance of techniques applied to the front but also from the side, it should be highlighted that they can be done two ways: only with the front foot, or with the movement of both.

In both situations rapidness and coordination are sought at the moment of impact. The steps may be short (the most used) but giant steps are also used with much success.

You must pay attention to the "landing" and see if the soles have taken the correct position.

F. TRICK TECHNIQUES

Trick techniques have as their main goal the diversion of attention that can be two ways:

1. Diversion of attention without contact and,
2. Diversion of attention with contact.

On referring to point 2, we must mention that contact may mean a grab of the hand, of the clothes etc.

A simple gesture made in the direction of the opponent will create a diversion of attention, a diversion that for a short time will have him distracted, in this short time or even at the same time that this lasts the real plan of attack has to be put into action.

Trick techniques are a good friend and are recommended to be used in confrontations with difficult opponents or in some cases with experts in a discipline of self defence, combat etc.

For a good performance of this technique you must assure yourself that the opponent is watching and reacts to your false actions, you must try it.

An important factor is the speed of the opponent's reaction to the false attacks, the real application of the chosen technique depends on this.

If it were not like this, setbacks may occur with undefined results and in such situations it is putting our skill, our speed of reaction and our knowledge to test.

If he is too uncommunicative and does not react to a false throw of a blow to the face, it must be tried again, if it does not work either then a breach must be opened in his defence, take him out of his "nest", make him open up.

The possibility also exists, it is almost an advantage for us, that if we are really going to attack and we haven't caused much diversion, we must continue, because if he is too uncommunicative this will work against him.

Look for the weak points, but be cautious.

If we find one of these types of behavior it is that the person in question is either too frightened, believes himself superior, or is simply preparing a surprise blow that he also hopes will be the only one, therefore break the shell carefully and eat the walnut bit by bit.

The trick technique may be composed of one or two actions followed and performed on different points of the opponent's anatomy, with or without movement, with or without getting too close, with more or less speed.

You must try your real plans before putting them into practice.

If it does not work, call me.

EXAMPLE OF TWO POSSIBLE WAYS OF TRICK TECHNIQUE

Getting close:
You must get close for your tricks to work.
Remember that the zone denominated as"safe" is considered to be 1.5 metres of distance between one of your extremities, usually the foot, and the most forward extremity of your opponent. To be able to apply the trick you must get close.
Getting close may be done by a slow and safe controlled approach, or with a rapid step towards your opponent which is a situation in which the grabbing of the hand or clothes is recommended. Getting close must be characterized by domination, apparent superiority, but always sure about what you are going to do. In the photo below, the approach has been done using one of the ways described above and the nearest element has been grabbed, the hand.
Our intention is not to apply a technique on the arm which is being held, this is the trick, and at the same time the deviation of attention.

Really we are going to apply a technique that has nothing to do with the arm but, apart from causing confusion and panic in the opponent, it is also useful to us as a control on his arm and indirectly on his concentration and focus.

Passing to the action we are going to show two possible actions taking the trick as the beginning of the attack.

The photo on the right shows us the continuation of the performance of a trick with a grab. Following the grab of the opponent's arm a front blow with step in front has been applied, in our case, on the throat, but it can be applied at any level and part of the body such as the testicles.
There are many cases in which I apply a kick technique directed to one of the feet with the aim of making him lose balance, fall over or simply with the effect of intermediary application, going again to the second diversion of attention.
To be able to have freedom of performance you must have the opponent's mind occupied as much time as possible, until the end. It is all a result of our tricks, attacks, movement actions, etc.
In the second example I am showing you the application of the trick by pushing the opponent's hand downwards followed by a blow to the chin. Both the trick as well as the blow have been applied with the same arm.

The trick has been done with a short movement of the right foot towards the opponent from the combat position, the body weight being distributed 60% on the front foot and 40% on the back.
The left hand is defending the chin and the elbow defending the stomach.

G. IMMOVILIZATION IN GRAB SITUATIONS

The technique in question refers to those street situations or others, (Judo, Hapkido techniques and others) from which we must escape. The techniques which will be shown next, TAUDANC techniques, implicate procedures related to locks, foot cuts, punches and the application of other techniques of the style with the aim of helping us to escape from situations of aggression and attacks be they street fights, demonstrations or championships.

We are going to try and give a solution to several situations applying specific TAUDANC techniques without entering into floor techniques which I will probably deal with in my 3rd book.

A grab situation is an annoying situation, threatening, preparatory of something bad that is going to happen and from which we have to get out of well. The techniques that are used I also recommend them to be used in defence against more than two attackers, are by immobilizing the first attacker and using him as a shield of defence against blunt objects or various attacks.

The grab situations applied by the attackers may be done from behind, in front, from the side, with both hands, with only one, grabbing the clothes, the hand or hands, or a mixture of both, grab of hand and clothes. From short distance attacks we are going to react, defending ourselves with defence techniques from the same category.

The examples which follow will be used to escape from these types of situations, but it must also be mentioned that there are many more techniques that can be used with the same purpose. From a certain point of view the grab can bring us advantages and I am referring to the control which we have mentioned in a previous chapter.

He, who grabs us is not aware of one very important thing which is: by grabbing something you are creating an immobile fixed point that the attacker thinks is advantageous only for himself because he began this action. This is totally mistaken. We also benefit from the creation of this stability and it gives us time to react by using, for example, precisely this fixed point, his hand or hands, because it would be ridiculous to grab us with the feet, it would leave too much room for action. Did you believe me?? I was just joking!!

So let's make the most of the attacker's lack of objectivity and let's try some techniques and see how they work. The "bridge" has been created, we have to break it, we no longer need to defend the safe distance zone, and without wanting to, we find ourselves involved in a fight of escaping, of attack, of defence to solve this annoying problem.

Next, a situation of **GRABBING WITH ONE HAND** and two different techniques being applied. Well, the expressions on each one of the faces will give you an idea. My son doesn't take it seriously, but he will see what happens next...

Well, analysis of the situation: one hand grabbing my clothes, the left hand prepared to hit. My position, normal. Opponent's grabbing arm semi bent, right foot in front, weight distribution of opponent 60% on the back foot, which tells me that a defence directed to the back would be very easy to do because it would help him to pass the remaining weight onto the front foot which is really holding the body up. But, you know, I will do even more, I will push him until he goes over the point of balance while I will make it possible to apply a technique towards the right and to the back. With this we have achieved that his left arm which was prepared to hit me cannot be used. Let's see.

Application of simple TAUDANC block to the inside of the opponent's elbow.

The hand that blocks pushes backwards and to the left (of the opponent). Grabbing with strength helps me apply the lock more effectively while my hand that is blocking is prepared (look at the direction of my hand) to push him backwards if necessary in a foot cut applied to his right foot.

Another technique applied at the same time of grabbing. Different because of my movement to the back, with the right hand break the grab or even better, grab the attacking hand at the same time that a direct blow is applied to the opponent, directing it to the front and down.

The application of this technique leaves the opponent unguarded at the same time that the action covers us. The movement to the back that we are going to do is begun at the hip, followed by the necessary and corresponding rotation of the body, and finally the right hand that can grab or break the opponent's hold has to be situated in a strong and stable position. In the pull applied at the moment of the turning of the body the right hand has positioned the opponent's hand exactly where the body has maximum stability.

GRAB WITH BOTH HANDS IN FRONT

We find ourselves in a very different situation from the one before because the opponent has done a double grab, (2 bridges to break). The next two examples will show us how to use the advantage of having the opponent's arms stuck to us and also his presence in our proximity that leaves the field clear for many techniques of foot cuts, let's see.

Action:
1. With both hands grab the arms of the opponent.
2. In one single movement the twist of the opponent's arms and the movement of our feet is applied until we are stuck to his chest and stomach with our back.
The opponent's arms are in a lock position.

Our hip opposes, for an instant, the carrying of the opponent's body until the opponent's weight is transferred higher up from our hip. In this precise instant we have total control and we can follow the application of the throwing technique.
3. By simply keeping perfect balance we continue turning to our left as much as necessary until the opponent falls.
One of the components of the performance is the "against action" with the hip. The feet slightly flexed so that at the moment of the turn they can be stretched out, raising the opponent's weight, giving the perfect touch to the technique. Another possibility of doing the technique is that of applying a foot cut together with the rotation and the lifting of the body of the opponent at the same time that our right foot is stretching out pushing to the back.
This happens when the opponent has already lost his balance (look at the opponent's left foot).
The stretch and push done by our leg may be applied at different heights.

There are so many techniques and ways of applying them that it is impossible to explain them all in several books. I have thought about it: 60% of what I can show would mean the total publication of 9-10 books, but we are also going to exist as a private entity where more things can be learnt, correct performances, awarding of titles by category for those who want to open their own school and give classes. But all this depends on you and on time, because each thing comes at its due time.

It is a new and unique style, the rest of them we already know and in my experience apart from the fact that the "product" has to be good, it also has to be new to be successful and to offer the satisfaction of novelty to the reader or the student.

What we are trying with the creation of private schools of TAUDANC-Spanish Martial Arts is to offer those people who are interested in really learning a new art of self defence, concentration, focus, breathing and much more. All this guaranteed with a title, awarded by the creator of this so marvelous art.

Well, to get back to what we were talking about, we must mention that the techniques applied in all types of defence against grabs can be mixed with the techniques that most suit, the certain moment and situation will determine the steps to be followed to escape from these annoying situations. However there are elements which should not be forgotten: a "bridge", grab, made by the opponent is as useful to you as he thinks that it is useful to him. The passive approach in which the opponent finds himself offers us only advantages. Many more dangerous grabs may exist, but each technique has its solution, the difference consists in many things: the level of preparation, the time of reaction of each one, weight, height, ground and other factors such as the dangerousness of the performance and its effects.

I consider that it does not make sense to defend ourselves by killing another person but instead teach him a lesson while we make ourselves safe.

TAUDANC should be looked at as a trade, because it can be considered as scientific fighting, studied and applied, tested and then again passing to a superior phase, carrying out a study applied on each one of the techniques, their effects and rest of components with participants that can be multiple.

Next we are going to present other solutions in grab situations or attempts of immobilization that can happen to each one of us at any given time of life. Another learning, another preparation that should in my opinion be included in all schools, just like the Japonese, Coreans, Chinese do ,as well as gym which is so limited but necessary.

As M.Tereza said:

"a teardrop in a lake will not do much, but how sad would the world be without this tear that contributes to fill the lake".

NECK GRAB

To get out of this situation we are going to apply first a lock technique on one of the opponent's fingers and secondly another lock applied on the opponent's elbow.
Usually both applications are done on the arm which is on top.

With the right hand one or more fingers are prized open or even the fist or the opponent's wrist. During the forced extension of the opponent's arm to the front we situate ourselves as far under his shoulder as possible. The result being: a fingers or wrist lock followed by an elbow lock or even a shoulder one.
The first thing to do after grabbing the finger or the wrist is to move the body to the right in such a way that the elbow or the upper part of the elbow ends up on our shoulder, supported and centered by the neck. The position of the legs are slightly bent so that in case of necessity they are able to take a higher position and widen the locks, together with the movement of the pull of the wrist to the front–down.
The right hand on grabbing and maintaining in lock position of practically three points of the opponent's arm, you have to squeeze the grabbed fingers very strongly.
If the opponent tries to escape, a change of body position to our left will make the performing of control even safer.

HAND GRAB

Even though my head is full of techniques that can be used to control the opponent I will show you an easy one. It gives good results and uses little body movement. The opponent's grab is not important if it is on top of or under the elbow, for the time being we have control of the situation, although he is not yet aware of this.
We can just observe that the position of the attacker is of a side nature and direction in comparison with our position which is normal, stable.
This is noticeable enough for the brain to put the TAUDANC techniques into action to get out of this situation which is trying to be rule.

The technique which we are going to apply to combat the created situation is a technique of OPEN ARMS with transfer of hands.
From our peaceful position we are going to perform the following movements:

1.The movement of the grabbed arm towards the left arm.
2.The lifting by the left arm of the opponent's arm and,
3.The application of one of the open arm techniques, which will consist in applying a blow-push on the opponent's neck and suitable change of position.

GRAB FROM THE BACK, (BEHIND)

In the situation created we find ourselves in a more difficult position than the previous ones, but even so we can obtain control, not only on the opponent's arms, but also on his whole body, applying the movement which suits us using TAUDANC techniques and our body weight. The Body Weight techniques are very special techniques which I am going to deal with in my next book. Returning to our present situation, the order of performance of the techniques and preparatory movements is:

1. Squeeze the attacker's left palm with our left palm so that it sticks to our body. In other words we are doing what he wants.
2. With the right hand we grab the opponent's right arm, if this is not possible we apply a strong squeeze with the elbow, immobilizing it by being stuck to us, with this we have arrived at the position of the proposed throw. The throw depends on us and we can apply it in two ways: 1. By throwing the opponent to the front letting him fall.
2. Throwing him to the floor at the same time that we let ourselves fall on top of him.
In this case our chin is always stuck to our chest.
In both cases the body weight, the throw to the front and the foot cut together with the corresponding rotation assure the correct performance.

GRAB OF CLOTHES WITH ONE HAND

Situation:
The opponent grabs our clothes with the left hand, we have instinctively grabbed his right arm with our left hand.
The technique which is going to be applied will be a lock on the opponent's left elbow.
Our left hand will push the opponent's right hand inwards until our right hand grabs and takes control of it.
During the transfer of hands our left hand performs a squeeze by grabbing the opponent's left hand and has it blocked in the same place that it already was, stuck to us.
From this position we continue by pushing as much as necessary to be able to obtain a severe lock on the opponent's arm.
The description of the strength of the arms is the following;
- the strength that the left arm applies in the grab is of 80%, while the strength applied on the right arm is between 30-40% and more if necessary.
Let us say that it is the strength that controls the immobility or the mobility of our opponent which is directed by us.
With this technique we are practically controlling our opponent entirely, and the distance in the case of a possible attempt of action.
By only raising our right arm we are making our opponent renounce any hostile action.
A lower position may be adopted if necessary.

GRAB OF CLOTHES WITH BOTH HANDS

Situation: double grab by the attacker at chest level, our position, inoffensive and normal. The difference from the previous examples is that the distance is shorter, the opponent's arms are semi bent applying considerable strength.

Well, this being the situation we are going to explain it: is a simple TAUDANC lock technique by twist of one of the arms.

This consists of an action without body movement applying a twist action on the right arm and a lock on the left arm.

Performance: The points on which the above named techniques will be are the opponent's elbows.

It begins with the application of a stable push upwards and towards the inside applied with our right palm on the elbow.

In a short time the opponent situates himself in a position in which the right elbow tends to open out.

In this instant, and a little after the performance of the first action, the lock is applied on the left elbow due to our action of pushing in and up.

Both movements are performed at the same time.

At the same time both movements will make the opponent fall over, or let go, or if he continues to grab even better.

We are going to move the right foot forwards and inwards and we will continue.

All techniques applied with the aim of immobilizing the attacker can be continued applying one or more TAUDANC techniques, doing this we are digressing from the name of the chapter but it is sometimes necessary.

I hope that in the next book I will have time to offer solutions and techniques that can follow on in the case of the opponent beginning to move, or simply if you do not want to continue having the opponent immobilized.

Really all types of TAUDANC techniques can be applied given the personal interest of the one who wishes to apply them to his opponent, be it a demonstration area or in a real street situation which, unfortunately, are present in all places and cities of the world.

But you have to start with something, so lets get to work, I could not say it better, let's get learning!

So we go on to the foot techniques that men like so much maybe because of the word foot or legs, I don't know, but let's see them.

5. MASTER FEET TECHNIQUES

A. KICKS .

B. BLOWS WITH THE KNEE .

KICKS

1. *Surprise / Joke Kick.*
2. *Direct Side Front Kick.*
3. *Short Direct/Front Kick.*
4. *Stop kick.*

BLOWS WITH THE KNEE

1. *Front Blow.*
2. *Side Blow.*

KICKS (CONTINUATION)

5. *Front Kick with Jump Step.*
6. *Front Kick to the Chin.*
7. *Simple Front* Kick.
8. *Side Kick with Simple Added Step.*
9. *Real Performances of Both.*
10. *Real Side Kick Performance with Jump Step, application at High Level.*
11. *Side kick with Jump.*
12. *"IN" Kick without Jump.*
13. *"OUT" Kick without Jump.*
14. *Kick to the back.*
15. *Kick to the back with Jump and Rotation.*
16. *Rotation Kick without Jump.*
17. *Ear Cut Kick.*
18. *"Cut off Air Supply" Kick.*
19. *Scissors Kick.*
20. *SIMPLE hook kick "Combed".*
21. *Hook Kick with Strength .*
22. *Hook Kick of medium Level.*
23. *Different Views of the Hooks, Simple and Strength.*
24. *Kicks with Jump and Turn.*

Sub Chapters

C. COMBINED MASTER TECHNIQUES.

D. DIRECT MASTER TECHNIQUES.

E. MASTER BLOCK TECHNIQUES.

F. MASTER PATCH TECHNIQUES.

G. MASTER " FOOT CUT " TECHNIQUES.

H. MASTER PRESSURE TECHNIQUES.

I. MASTER BUTT TECHNIQUES.

J. MASTER THROWS.

L. MASTER DODGES.

M. MASTER ATTACKS.

N. MASTER BULTER TECHNIQUES .

O. MASTER OPPRESIVE TECHNIQUES.

5. MASTER FEET TECHNIQUES

A. KIKS, B. BLOW WITH THE KNEE,

Good afternoon, I have just finished doing the housework to help my wife who is very busy with my son of 3 and half months, well, where did we leave it off ? Oh yes, let's continue...

Master Feet Techniques are a composition of techniques performed with the feet and his components. There are techniques developed by me and there are techniques that can be found in many Martial Arts. Even so, the action is specific of TAUDANC. I realize that seen briefly, some can say that a side kick is a side kick and it is done the same way in all the styles. And I say to you, it is not true and I will repeat what I said in the first book, no two performances are the same even if tried by the same person. I will go even further by saying, that only the focus before the application, of whichever kick, is different.
The muscular tone changes the same way that the concentration and distribution of strength changes, why if not, in martial arts films do even the best ones have to repeat various takes? To be able to gather all the components and use them at one same time, that's what I call art!

Apart from this, each person has his own style of performance, each one understands in a different way with a different profoundness, we are not all the same, thank goodness, how boring, if all of us were the same...

In the end, millions of students can and know how to perform a side kick learnt in a country "X", in a club "X" but they will never be the same in performance. You can test this with your colleagues, it does not matter if they have had the same teacher and have received the same formation and information.

There will always exist an unwitting peculiarity of performance, instinctively cultivated, evaluated and maintained, that with time may suffer modifications more or less important; so peculiarity exists in each one of us. In my opinion peculiarity is good, it marks the difference between individuals of the same race and gets the good and less good or the worst out of each person, it is practically the personalization of a person.

Next we will see performances of TAUDANC style and I hope that soon you will be able to at least see the first DVD so that you can also understand TAUDANC in movement and be able to make an opinion, having a greater vision on everything that I have told you about peculiarity. All the demonstrations have been done using protection equipment and at no time has 100% strength and full capacity been used so that nobody has been hurt or injured.

SURPRISE KICK

Starting from the combat position we approach the opponent at a distance which is considered to be optimum for the performance of this technique.
It needs to diminish the so called safe distance just as described in a previous chapter and corresponds to 1.5 m of distance between the exterior extremities of both participants. It is a foot technique of middle and short distance and is characterized by the rare path that the action takes as well as the surprising strength that can be used in the application. It is a technique which I am very fond of and I will tell you why:
- It takes the opponents by surprise.
- It uses much strength transmitted by the hip.
- The action hides the body.
- It has many possibilities of application of techniques.
- It has an easy performance.
- There is the possibility of combining with a hand grab.
- It has a tendency to trick because the majority of people's lack of knowledge, and I will stop here.

The action uses the side part of the foot as the point of impact.
A light movement to the front has been used at the moment of action together with the grabbing of the opponent's hand. The grab is indicated but not obligatory.
The technique is applied with the foot which is bent during the performance.

DIRECT KICK TO THE SIDE

For the performance of this technique we need to get closer to the opponent if we are not already at a corresponding distance. Getting closer can be done by the added or jumped step and in this case the application of the kick must follow as soon as possible, without giving the opponent time to think or react. It may be applied with or without movement. The foot which will apply the blow in this case and usually, is the front one. The most important thing in the performance is the correct application of the foot's path and the part of the foot that will make impact on the opponent's abdomen. If we explain it in parts we have: the getting closer (if necessary), the raising of the knee, of the foot that applies the blow, to waist level. This will be accompanied and performed in one action with the moving of the foot towards the opponent's abdomen. You must be very careful with body rocking. Body rocking has to be premeditated, preparing in this way the foot's correct path. We are going to need to assure the rocking whether it be for the raising of the foot and opening out or, to prepare the corresponding rocking at the moment of impact. The body has to be prepared to maintain its balance even after impact. The path is straight at the beginning, followed by the total opening out of the foot, the blow being applied to the side and up.

We have to mention that all movements need the correct change of position of the supporting sole, beginning with a light raising of the heel followed by the movement propelled by the hip indicating the direction to follow and take.
I know that it seems simple but it isn't and it is very important, influencing not only the body's balance but also performance, avoiding accidents etc.
But hey, this is a book for those who are advanced, so those who practise already know it and those who don't, let them practise!

SHORT DIRECT KICK

Consists in the moving of the foot in a quick to and fro movement.
It may be applied either with the front foot or the back foot.
I recommend it with the front foot, in this way diverting attention and following quickly with other techniques and combinations.

The blow is applied with the outside part of the toes of the performing foot, maintaining and coordinating the balance and the strength generated by the hip.
This must be of medium intensity given the fact that it is only a short distance application without too much movement and it does not need to use the propelling movement of the hip 100%.
It is recommended to be used in blows directed to the testicles, the feet, and knees and generally in medium height blows below the belt.
In the photo a front application can be seen but the opponent may have a side position and although I recommend the front application it may be applied on the opponent's front foot in the higher and lower parts of the knee.
You always have to adapt to the existing situation until bit by bit you get to be the creator of the situations that you want, corresponding to the techniques for which they have been created.
It has been tested and works very well as a trick and also as a real action in combination with a direct blow of the Elastic Hand, and other techniques of the Open Hands.

STOP KICK

The aim of the kick is to bring down the opponent using two ways of application depending on what you wish to obtain: the bringing down or the confusing of the opponent together with the loss of balance thus creating a positive position for the following applications.
It may be done from any base position and the use of force depends on what we have mentioned above. It can be applied with 100% strength for the bringing down of the opponent and it can be applied as a single blow with one quick to and fro movement, the withdrawal being at a normal speed. In the action the knee is not raised as in other techniques, the foot has a rising path from the floor to the back part of the opponent's knee. Once here, the blow changes direction and goes down. However in the second situation you only kick and withdraw. In both situations the foot makes a semicircle and the blow is applied with the sole of the foot. You will have discovered that I have also applied a grab before applying the technique. It must be a professional habit formed from my childhood times when I was still practising Judo. Well, it is very useful to me.
So try not to let them grab you.
It can be applied in the same way either with the foot in front or with the foot at the back.
What I recommend is that: to be applied with our back foot, creating space due to the long movement.

BLOWS WITH THE KNEE

Knee blows although very useful in short distances do not represent a technique of great importance in TAUDANC.
Even so, we use them as blows, as blocks or like a preparatory action for the application of other techniques. In the photo an attack with added step has been performed or what we call an entrance, with the knee directed to the opponent's side at the same time that the opponent's right arm has been moved away, therefore having partial control of it. The knee blow may be applied practically on any part of the body situated in the upper part with or without grab, with or without jump step, with or without a jump, or as an entrance or secondary part in a confrontation. But listen to this : As famous as some Martial Arts are we forget the most important thing which is that "the shirt is always closer than the jacket", meaning that man has created a multitude of combinations and of possible blows, some spectacular (for those who adore shows and films) and we are distracted being robbed of reality.

And the reality is, that a knee blow applied to the genitals, such an old blow and so often used even by our grandfathers and ladies, has been forgotten about.

In my opinion it is a diversion of provoked attention, proposed by several great masters. In TAUDANC we consider it an important technique without stopping the application of the others, given the particular and unique character of each situation of confrontation, but, first things first.

Next we are going to see some demonstrations of this technique without reproducing the ancient knee blow to the genitals which is very well known.

Therefore we have the opportunity to judge for ourselves the efficiency and the risk of performance of each one and all the applications related to the knee blow.

Avoid complication, look for simplicity.

Good, lets go there.

FRONT KNEE BLOW

Applied to the stomach from the back towards the front. The foot leaving from the back bends on the way.
Very useful in grab situations of short distance.
In the performance body rocking is used towards the back as much as needed maintaining the necessary stability for future applications of continuation techniques. The knee, when applying knee blow techniques can have various levels of impact and most importantly, various directions.
Therefore, in the picture an upwards path has been applied with an applied strength of 50%, the support foot being the foundation pillar on which all the remaining weight is supported, something which makes it fundamental to defend.

SIDE BLOW WITH KNEE

By custom or necessity knee blows are all applied using the back foot. It is so that the throw that is needed can be applied with force. Apart from the disadvantage of using a short tool, it is also "announced" that something is coming towards the opponent.
It is also true, however, that it is a technique that does not deserve to be left to one side but to be remembered, to be used in short distance fights or blocking attacks or simply to keep the distance.

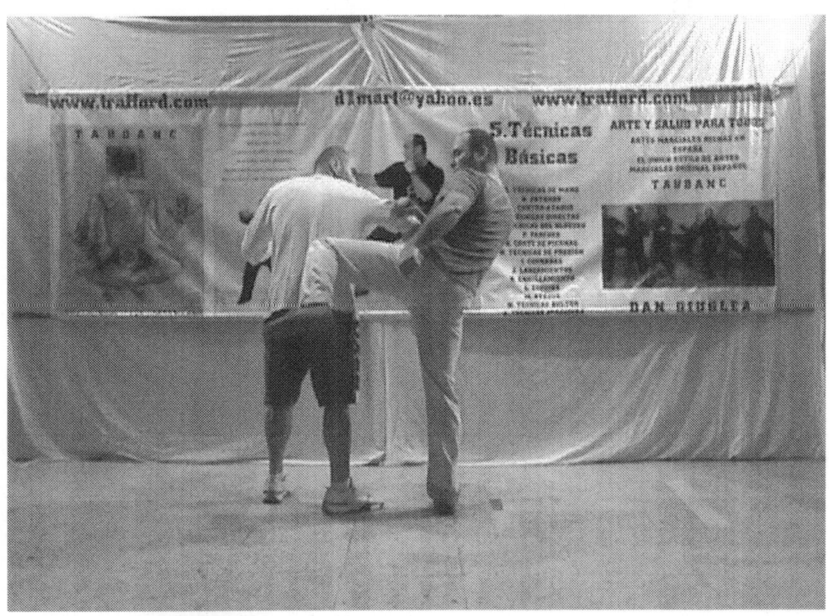

FRONT KICK WITH JUMP STEP

It begins by changing the side combat position to the front, together with the front and upwards movement of the left arm which makes the counter weight, together with the rocking of the body towards the back.
The raising of the arm can also be used as a trick.
Next, the transfer and maintaining of the weight and the stored strength on the support foot is made, in our case the right foot.
With all these elements stored and prepared we carry out the movement towards the opponent while we raise the knee as much as necessary for the application of the kick.
All of the body must act like a machine, the left foot is prepared to move.
The jump step is done by moving the front foot further forwards with a small parallel jump and very close to the ground for quick action.
Pay attention at all times to the opponent.
As we approach the opponent, the knee rises and the body goes to the back to assure the rocking.
The left arm begins to lower to a certain point, helping the application of the concentrated forces, about to be freed on the opponent's abdomen, by the heel or the knuckles of the toes of the left foot which are facing forwards.

We continue with the total movement of the left foot and the discharging of all the stored energy, energy which will be controlled by the expelled air and the withdrawal of the left foot as it is moved, the foot's path being the opposite to the left arm. The hip pushes the foot inwards and forwards in one

single movement. I know that the components that intervene in a correct performance are many but, believe me, you are on the right road. Look at the position of the support foot, it is supported by the toe knuckles and it will move a little more to the front. This small distance which is applied by changing the position to the front by several centimeters, makes the blow destructive. Observe how the foot has penetrated the opponent's abdomen and has really lifted it from the floor. Look how the opponent bends when he receives the discharging of my energy at the exact moment and the exact point, he is practically flying. And he flies more meters to the back. It is a technique of strength, not a to and fro application. I won't make any comments because the photograph speaks for itself. The withdrawal of the foot is done slowly after the strong impact. At the same time it is controlling the opponent's path.

This is a little difficult to explain but it is like this, that somehow, by looking at the toes, you can see the path and its effect, which is the perfect performance.

The withdrawal and taking of position. Making a general study we can easily observe the taking of position, with the left arm prepared for a possible intervention, the right arm still lining up strength and the correct rocking position. The foot which has performed the technique is placed in front in a comfortable position.

You enjoyed that didn't you??? Well me too and I have been doing it for many, many years. This is only a demonstration without concentration and without total use of the mental and physical components. It is also true that given that it is a demonstration the opponent is not in a mental state of fight or defence. All the same, this is the action that has to be applied when it is a front kick to the middle zone of the body, be it abdomen, stomach or solar plexus.

You have to practice much to reach these results. Years is the right term or measurement element that describes the needed time.

FRONT KICK TO THE CHIN / FACE

From the position that we have described previously the same movement is applied but in this case it is a high blow in which it is necessary to increase the rocking during the upwards movement of the foot together with good breathing and a suitable movement to be able to have strength.

In the second part of the action the strength and the conduct of the body are already established.
The support foot is prepared to transmit the "grain" of strength.
Depending on what you wish to achieve the impact may be direct with a rapid to and fro action or it can be applied with a forward and upwards path .

In the second option much more strength will be used, and the movement will be wider. Meanwhile, in the first option, we opt for the powerful and rapid impact that is obtained due to the small point of impact and which lacks the combined application of the blow and push. It is logical that on pushing we need supplementary rocking to the back, as for the first option we don't. The third part shows us the moment following the impact, the effect of the applied force and the path taken by the used object. This to and fro action was chosen considering that the reader can easily understand the other application but at a high level. There are the same characteristics as the front kick with jumped step where the blow - push is applied.
The difference is clear. If you don't see it clearly and you still have the book at hand have a look at the chapter in question, or put your glasses on!
Well, hoping that I have disconnected you a little, let's go on to the following application.

SIMPLE FRONT KICK

We call it simple because the performance does not need any type of movement.
It can be carried out in the same way either with the front foot or with the back foot with differences between them.
When you strike with the back foot it is advisable to apply the blow-push.

As for the performance using the front foot, it is recommended that you use strength applied in a rapid to and fro movement.
In such cases it is not necessary the use of body rocking being in the majority of cases a simple action with good results in short and middle distances.
The distribution of body weight is also different in both applications, using more in the blow-push which also requires the increase of the rocking to the back.
In the photograph we can again observe the position in which the left arm is found once the blow is applied.
Please pay attention to the straight line made by my foot which applies the blow as well as the position of the soles facing to the right.

Of much importance also is the position of the support foot that is a little bent, position imposed by the correct and so necessary balance, a balance that absorbs part of the impact without losing any stability.
It is a whole, like the entire body, that has to be maintained in all the techniques.

SIDE KICK WITH ADDED STEP AND SIMPLE SIDE KICK

So as not to repeat the last 2 photos we have first put the performance with added step which also contains the simple performance. And lets go on to the performance. From base position the body is prepared for movement towards the opponent by an added step which is going to move towards the opponent.
The right hand has been stretched, a little more than the normal combat position, pointing towards the point of impact while the necessary distance is maintained for the application of the technique. When I say the preparation of the body, I refer to the taking of position of the photo with the back straight, suitable breathing and preparing the expelling of corresponding air at the moment of impact. The second part consists of taking the correct position and with perfect balance moving the left foot TROUGH THE BACK (one of the great errors that can be made is to move the foot trough front).
Pay attention to the position of the body facing a little to the right looking at the photo.
The feet are semi bent without touching each other giving the following movement in which the left foot will extend to the maximum.
In this precise instant thoughts should not exist, the performance of the technique will be natural with all the focus that the TAUDANC student can use.

The following step consists in raising the right foot at the same time as the rising of the body, stretching out the feet.
Depending at which height you want to apply the blow, the right knee will be raised more or less. In the present performance it is to the abdomen.

The arms have now taken another position; the right arm in defence or application of knuckle blow if something unexpected happens, while the other arm apart from being prepared to defend also assures the balance. The invisible diagonal which should be formed between the raised foot and the left arm rests on the vertical balance formed by the whole body, with the base on the left foot which at the moment does not have maximum extension. Between the two a perfect balance is created suitable for controlled movements. Let's continue with the 4th action of performance, but before, I want to remind the reader that everything that they have seen in these four photos is only the detailed demonstration in parts. The performance in itself will be seen next. So, just as the foot is moving, the right arm moves energetically to the back until landing on the performing foot. This movement is directly connected to the movement of the left arm and the total extension of the support foot. The last two photos show the simple side kick in detail.

REAL PERFORMANCE OF SIDE KICK WITH OR WITHOUT ADDED STEP APPPLIED AT MIDDLE LEVEL.

We had to do the demonstration in parts to be able to be caught on camera and to maintain the maximum height of the performers for an improved view. I don't know if I have managed it as an amateur but this is how they have come out.

Well, here is the effort.

Don't think it is easy, it's not when you do it yourself.

REAL PERFORMANCE OF SIDE KICK WITH JUMPED STEP (SKIP) APPLIED AT HIGH LEVEL

The difference between side kick with step added and that with jumped step is the jumped step. It is not a jump, it is a step done by jumping. There is a great difference between them as there is also a difference in the performance of the side kick with JUMP, in which really the jump is used before the application of the blow. I can confirm that the jumped step is really the action of the added step with the addition of maximum speed. I recommend that you control the effect of the blow as well as the supervision of the opponent, maintaining control of the situation to be able to decide what can be expected from the opponent after this blow. It is also important to make the most of the situation depending on each individual case.

SIDE KICK WITH JUMP
(ALL THE PHOTOS WITHOUT TRICKS)

Telling jokes before performing is not bad, but only after 26 years of activity.
It is a good technique to surprise the opponent.
It has one bad thing though: you need much practice to be able to laugh and focus on the performance at the same time.
Step one: position,
Step two: jump,
Step three: strike,
Step four: land.
Pay much attention to the landing so as to avoid accidents and damage to the ankle and knee.
It must be practised many times but slowly, without hurry, with breathing pauses and relaxation of the muscles.
The practice of several high jumps without applying the blow is indicated before the full performance.
Impact blow without push.

THE " IN " KICK WITHOUT JUMP

The "IN" kick is characterized by the semicircle which describes the action of this technique.
The movement is from the outside towards the inside. The performance can be of two types:
1. With the foot totally straight at the moment of impact and,
2. With the foot semi bent a case in which the blow is applied with the sole of the foot applied to the face.
In the 1st option, the blow is applied with the opposite part of the sole and is used at a long distance, the difference being that the 2nd option is used at middle and short distance.
In the photos the first option is shown. The foot drags everything in its path and in the final point of the performance it ends up on the floor. The moment that the foot touches the target additional strength is applied as a circular push downwards to the floor.

THE " OUT " KICK WITHOUT JUMP

Unlike the "IN" kick, the "OUT" kick is applied using the front foot. It begins by bringing the back foot close to the front foot, centering all the body weight on the right foot. Situated in this position we pass to the performance of the bending and moving of of the foot. The technique, the same as the previous one, traces a semi circle. The movement of the foot is produced while the foot is following its circular path towards the outside, in our case the left. The hands make the counter weight for the performance, while the foot touches its target. It already finds itself in a contrary movement to that of the left arm which helps the driving of the blow. The use of the arm is recommended.

BACK KICK

Just as the name indicates it refers to a performance of a kick with the opponent situated to the back of us. First we turn the head to locate the opponent followed by positioning ourselves at the corresponding distance for the application to have effect. Next we raise the right knee above the hip. At this moment, gathering all the necessary elements including measured breathing, we pass to the performance of the technique that, together with the turn of the head towards the opponent, the movement is prepared with the afferent discharge of strength.

The next step is to put all the effort into a maximum opening of both feet, applying the kick at the level and strength desired.

Even though all the strength and a perfect performance has not been used, the cause and effect can be seen perfectly.

BACK KICK WITH JUMP AND ROTATION

Unlike the previous performance the starting position is facing the opponent, point in which we prepare the body for the jump that will be applied at the same time as the rotation and the blow.
The three elements are performed at the same time. I am not going to repeat the other components mentioned in each previous chapter.
Pay attention to the movement of the opponent's feet and body.
At the moment of impact, the body is freed of the accumulated energy onto the opponent's body.
The support foot should be straight. But I'm past 44, I'm sure that younger ones will do it better.

There is no greater joy for a Master than his pupil being better than his teacher.

TURNING KICK WITHOUT JUMP

Combat position taken at the suitable distance for the performance, followed by the body turn started by the hip and continued by the body, the arms stretched out. The foot which performs the blow is the one situated at the back.
In photo number two the position of the body, already prepared for the throw as can be seen, is applied by the push and rotation of the hip, but it will not have the effect of power that it should have without the rotatory bend of the body forwards, as in photo no three. We have 3 physical components.
1. the hip, 2, the bend of the body towards the front and 3, the body weight on the right foot. From here the foot applies all the force in a wide turning path. To follow the performance follow the changes of position of the opponent and you will learn what has not been said.

EAR CUT KICK

The kick that is demonstrated is well known as Mawashi Geri in the majority of karate styles such as, “despacho” in Thai boxing and Round House Kick in other arts. Well, ours is called Ear Cut and presents a difference, a peculiarity in comparison with the rest of the mentioned arts.

This difference consists in the semi circle with a very small radius therefore cutting the time and the distance. The performance is rapid, intrepid and reaches the opponent’s ear to return in one or two moments to the initial combat position.

Believe me, I know what I am saying and I know the results of all my experiences and rehearsals. I can apply it by starting from a position with the feet, one near the other in line, while the others need the foot to perform a very wide semi circle (waste of time and energy). From very far back, I began with Karate Shotokan (Nakayama´s Books), I began to learn and I liked Karate Ghioku Sinkay and then I continued with Wado Riu, the rest I will tell you in my next book.

To see the impact look at photo number five and then think how it should be done to give you time to put your foot back in initial position.

CUT OFF AIR SUPPLY KICK

The same technique applied at medium level, to the abdomen or solar plexus or in some part of the middle depending on whether the opponent's position is totally to the side or not.

With the risk of repeating myself I ask you to look at photo number two, to see exactly how to apply the arm movement in an opposite direction to the performing foot.
The left arm is pulling an imaginary string tied to the left arm and the ankle, also left. Well, for a good performance think of the imaginary string and you will do it well.

The application of the blow also includes the to and fro movement at maximum speed, and the blow has a strictly impact character without any type of push. You must try to use the final part of the performance and I refer to the instant in which the foot has already applied the blow and is prepared to withdraw. In this precise moment a very short push with little strength is applied but not with the effect of a push; but to help the foot to use the force of the rejection generated by the part which has been hit for a rapid withdrawal.

Looking at the last photo, somebody moved.

SCISSOR KICK

The scissors kick is characterized by copying exactly the movement of a pair of scissors while they are cutting. There is an exception, one that is demonstrated in the photographs on the right which is applied in middle and short distance and there is a performance of long distance, which better describes the cutting movement of scissors. It begins by organizing the application which consists in raising the foot which is NOT going to apply the blow but will help the performing of this action. The 2nd part consists in making the jump followed by the application of the blow with the left foot. If it is applied at short or medium distance the total extension of the foot which applies the technique is necessary together with the application of a small push to the front so that the opponent's head goes in the direction indicated by the pushing foot, which is to the back.

Normally the performance is in two parts but both parts also have different performances.

1st situation:

- The performance is one single action of raising the opposite foot to the one which will apply the blow together with the jump, and the second part is described as the single application of the blow with or without a push by the other foot.

2nd situation:

- The performance of raising the foot followed by the second part which will be the application of the blow together with the performing of the jump.

In all the situations the base element and the promoter of the correct performance is the exact movement of scissors that, if looking at it more closely, what is it that they do? The two components change position more or less at the same time. Well this being the principal, we have to practise, discovering the movement of a pair of scissors which are standing up, discover the point of balance, the suitable distance for each sub technique, long, medium and short.

The movement in its entirety has to be studied and practised and the way of applying the push as the end of the performing foot extension. The most difficult part is the application of the small push of the opponent's head with the extremities of the foot which is applying the scissors technique, but nothing is impossible, I can assure you, if you learn the components well, the actions, their purposes, their cycle of performance, amongst so many other things that intervene in a TAUDANC technique and in life. Also the basic scissors once learnt have a very special application which is the application in the final part, the application of the blow to the inside or outside, but if I tell you everything I will not have much to tell you in the next book, so for the time being get scissoring!

In the performance, for a short time the body will not be in contact with the floor, much care, in this moment you are vulnerable, don't let the opponent act. Each action has to have its own result, each movement its plan and path. Don't apply the techniques without being sure of their good application and effect.

All the jumps or the majority of them share a measure of risk, beginning with the necessary time for their performance, but this has also a solution; a side or front kick with applied jump always from an suitable distance which has been practised and proved does not have a risk given its good performance and its being well known backed up by the effective practice of the same.

Don't leave yourselves uncovered, and if you are not sure of something, go on to the application of a more suitable technique for this precise instant but always remember that "you and your enemy are one", without him you can not do anything so keep close but distant.

SIMPLE HOOK KICK "COMBED"

The Simple Hook Kick "combed", has as an active element, the semicircle traced by the performing foot, to and fro, applied during the ascending of the foot towards its target. The to and fro in reality is performed by the knee's movement followed by the picking up of the foot bringing it into a position X totally bent. The performance may be done in steps or one single step. As for the performance in steps these are:

1. The performance of the added step moving the right foot towards the opponent and resting it behind the left foot (photo Nº2),
2. Use the knuckles of the toes of the right foot as a support and centre of body weight and the rising to and fro action of the left foot.
3. The technique describes a blow with the aim to hit 25% of the outside of the opponent's head, it is considered a simple blow without use of sufficient strength to bring down the opponent.
4. Performance in one single step:

Consists in the interchange of position of the feet described above in one single action, included in this is the application of the blow and withdrawal, all in one action that in reality is a low jump with interchange of positions.

HOOK KICK WITH STRENGTH

The application of this technique in particular implies the carrying out of a rising movement of narrowness (of the semicircle) compared with the one described previously. Given its particular movement care must be taken to not drag or touch the opponent's hand or any exterior part. Our target is the opponent's head or neck. The application of the blow begins once the foot has been thrown applying to it a hip movement full of strength in the path from down towards the side. While this is happening the body finds itself twisted between the foot which is going to the front and the arm which is going in the opposite direction. The arms having an essential influence in the transmission of the received and transmitted strength.
It is a blow of strength.

As much as I want to explain each technique it is impossible to describe totally, for this I am adding on some performances as a demonstration for a better understanding of each detail. For this I am thinking about creating a private school of TAUDANC Spanish Martial Arts with courses, even long distance courses, and examinations after a period of study. The educational material will be my books, my videos and the attendance of practices before the examination or during the necessary time until obtaining the title of Master, therefore the people who wish to open their own school may do so.
But don't forget, it is all of a private nature, by this I mean that no federation will recognize your titles (nor do we need to), each Master having his own school.

Going back to the book, I recommend that, apart from all the explanations that I am giving, you always study the photos well, especially the opponent's behavior because, although having all the protective elements he describes the corresponding movements of the applied technique, he shows you the position in which he were in at the beginning and during the performance and the final moment of the performance of each technique.
Something very important is the study of the opponent's face and eyes, the look, that is, the look can tell us many things but, so as to recognize what is going to happen before, first you have to practise to be able to recognize the start of each technique. You must always be aware of your opponent even when you find something wrong in his position or in his defence or attack to be able to act sure and on time.

You must be alert but relaxed because you can't lose any opportunity that is offered to you, I can assure you, there are many.
Your tactics must be made up of trickery, of taking advantage, control and action.
Punish your opponent's mistakes but respect him, create breaks in his defence, break his guard, don't let him think, open yourself a path, or let him subconsciously leave you the space that you need to apply your techniques.
Adapt yourself as much as possible to his style, study him as much as possible, even in parts, and once his game has been learnt put into action your knowledge, show him what is speed, strength, reflexes and all other techniques. The time of power will arrive, expose yourself and apply series of learnt TAUDANC techniques but first learn to learn, know your enemy, take him "out for a walk", study him and you will win.
The majority of people are 100% preoccupied with applying their techniques, give him time and false opportunities and you will know more about your opponent, or simply make use of your knowledge at suitable times. Respect your opponent and he will respect you, fight but control the fight.

HOOK KICK MIDDLE LEVEL

The performance is the same as the simple or with strength hook kick with the indication that the point of impact is situated at medium level of the human body,
In photo nr. one, the right foot has already been placed behind the foot that in the beginning was in a forward position. It is an advance towards the opponent in a side position created by putting the right foot behind the left.
From here the technique is applied at the previously named level, the path of the blow can be direct towards the back or direct impact with a small withdrawal, finalizing with the withdrawal. In 3rd photo we wanted to show the performance with strength with the blow applied in a back direction, in such a case the stomach is hit, the position of the foot is in a comfortable and advantageous position but taking into account the possible opposition of the opponent, and I refer to the partial abdominal contraction of the opponent, something which would change the path of the withdrawal of the performing foot.

DIFFERENT VIEWS OF SIMPLE AND STRENGHT HOOKS

On the right, simple hook kick to the abdomen, below, the previous photo of the application of the hook.

Below, hook in force, medium level.

KICKS WITH JUMPS AND ROTATION

Next I will demonstrate the necessary steps for the performances of many techniques applying the jump together with rotation.
Combat position as starting position, we are going to perform a jump and a complete rotation to the left, Photo no 1.
The following photograph shows the position taken after the rotation with jump and the preparation of the following movement.
The following step consists of the jump with applied rotation which will help us in the performance of many techniques such as : "IN" Kick, "OUT" Kick, Side Kick, Hook Kick and several more that are done with one foot or the other.

This is a very important factor in the performance of techniques with jumps and rotations, depending on which foot is going to be used and which technique a surplus of energy, speed and height will be needed.
You must know which foot is going to be used from the combat position due to the fact that in one performance more speed is used and in the other more strength but both are characterized by the jump with rotation.

C. COMBINED MASTER TECHNIQUES

The combined master techniques use several combinations of advanced techniques whether foot or hand together with the specific steps and movements corresponding to TAUDANC.

They may be composed of hand and foot techniques alternating amongst themselves. They may also be applications of series of three blows each one, techniques performed with rotations, with grabs, with blocks, throws to the floor, butts and other techniques that each real defence situation imposes.

Practically, combinations can be created or performed that best suit or adapt to the situation, or those that are wanted to be used, those that are most liked if the situation allows or those that most adapt to the skills of the student.

Next I am going to present some so that the reader or student can have a starting point and it can help him to understand the principles of the combined master techniques to which this technique refers, its good interpretation and learning.

The most simple techniques have been chosen to be combined with other techniques of a superior manner and level to that described and shown in the first book "TAUDANC SELF DEFENCE AND HEALTH" published in August 2007. This has as its aim the introduction to TAUDANC without being about techniques or explanations of an advanced level, but taking into account the necessary parameters for a simple learning forming the foundations of the student.

In the following pages appropriate attention must be paid not only to the applications but also to the movements which are associated to each technique.

It will be of much use to the reader helping him as well as giving him a general idea about the techniques, also about each movement in particular etc.

It is now time that the student appreciates or recognizes the weight distribution, the percentage of strength application, the direction in which to fall or to move the opponent as each photo shows.

It is a simple recognizing of what has been learnt, the reading of this book, of the capacity of learning and the motor development of the reader or student. On seeing each technique being applied, remember that it is only a printed demonstration and try to imagine the real performance in a real situation, the cause and effect of each movement or thought that has been used for the carrying out of the techniques which are presented as follows.

COMBINATION Nº I

Elements of multiple combinations. Photos 5.

Defence carried out with the palm inwards at the same time that the front blow at medium level is applied.
Application of corresponding bend.
Next the right hand applies a side blow with the knuckles at the same time that the position changes towards the left.
The right foot in its movement closes in as much as necessary to the opponent.
Photo number three shows us the continuation, considered logical, but it is not the only application of the Butt technique at medium level.
The direction of the application can be to the side or to the back.
The shoulder hits while the right knee blocks.

Applying the block or not of the opponent's left foot and considering that the Butt has been applied as a blow without the specific push, we can continue with the application of the foot cut technique to the front, contrary to the movement of the right arm. The opponent being in an uncontrolled situation we can follow with the application of the second foot cut, this time applied on the right foot and to the front. The right arm grabbing the clothes or the arm of the opponent pulling in the same direction.

The right foot can apply a foot cut with hook on the opponent's right foot to reduce the time of performance of the combination and to mark the end with the falling down of the opponent. In this case the fall of the opponent will be directed by the cut with hook that has a semi circle performance towards the back and the right looking at the photo; by which the opponent will fall to the left side also looking at the photo, which corresponds to the right one of the performer.
The combination can be reduced to two or three elements depending on the situation created and the desired effect at the right moment.
We have performed a combination of five parts to give the reader more possibilities of study either by, learning the techniques seperately, or only the first or the last and finally, so that he can choose that which he most considers adapts to his possibilities and skills.

Combination Nº1A

Photos 5.

**In defence the block of the blow has been applied to the outside while the blow has been applied to the genitals.
It has been done in front position.**

Next, one of the Open Arms Techniques has been applied to the opponent's neck without changing position. Observe in both photos the bend of the opponent, and the position of the feet which shows best the following of the received blow.

**Combination number three consists of the application of elbow blow from up-downwards adding to it a push to the right so that the opponent separates.
Comparing the photos nº2 and nº 3 it can easily be seen the change of position.**

The taking of the corresponding position is next for the application of one of the blows.
The application of the blow with the knuckles created by the withdrawal and then the deploy of the arm.
The elbow in its application of the blow goes downwards, from here the Elastic Hand Technique is applied expressed by the uppercut applied to the chin.
And finally, the application of a Butt propelled by the natural movement to the right applied with the right shoulder blade or the back.
The application of the butt is done by moving the right foot in a semicircle, putting it into line with the opponent's right foot at the same time that the right arm takes the suitable position for the application of the butt.
In this instant the body curves and bends towards the opponent with the distribution of weight to the back and the right foot a little bent.
I don't know if you will understand exactly what I am going to explain but: the whole of all the movements that intervene in the performance of the butt generates a movement of impact similar to a tremble that is transmitted to the opponent by the shoulder in the culminating moment of the leaning of the body and the light flexing of the right foot. To obtain a greater effect the created lean can be increased together with the reduction of the distance of performance.

The photos are nice, the techniques are too, and I like Martial Arts films but: DO NOT be fooled, a demonstration is a demonstration and a real defence situation is nothing like the films or nice photos.

I have said many times even in the first book, that what I have shown in my books may be applied without problems but the order of performance, the choosing of the technique, the reflex actions and other components that intervene in real situations have to be the first factors of attention for the TAUDANC student.

Remember this: in a demonstration the opponent is instructed and advised on which technique will be applied, apart from which, this the opponent is not an opponent but a person who is helping in a demonstration without responding, counter attacking or following any thought process. Practising with the punch bag or other training tool is good and recommended but the punch bag will never return the punches so it won't be the same as defending yourself from a real attacker.

The combinations shown are of much use and really in a real situation it is enough to correctly apply a technique, only one to end the combat without damages or scratches. Apply the technique which best adapts to the situation and when training think of a real opponent, controlling your instincts, do not give away your plans (that don't exist) to your opponent, offer him only surprises, don't give him time to guess what you are going to do. Constantly change distance and position, alternate the apparently firm taking of position, face up to the attacks from your opponent. Answers have to be given or avoided, there are things to do, to guess.

COMBINATION Nº 2

Multiple elements, photos 4.

Block of Direct Techniques with lock against blow directed to the face taking position to the left side. We have led the opponent to the place and necessary position for the next application of techniques. The opponent's balance, weak.

This position has been arrived at starting from the combat position and together with the application of the necessary body rotation the block has been performed. The right foot which in combat position can have a forward position or not, has made an advance towards the opponent situating itself the nearest to the opponent to apply the necessary force to the block and to prepare the next movement or change of position for the application of the following technique. With or without movement of the right foot we are going to pass on to the following performance. This consists of the turning of the opponent's arm with the palm upwards and the application of a kick to the already extended elbow or even better, below the shoulder. While all this occurs the mind has already prepared the following technique which is going to be applied with all its components.

The third performance consists of the application of an elbow blow to the ribs on the right side of the opponent. The blow is performed at the same time that the left foot touches the floor, to all this the strength transmitted by the bend of the body towards the opponent must be added. It is a firm position. As can be seen, the grab of the hand has been maintained for better control and to maintain the opponent's mind distracted towards the grab, while we are going to apply other techniques to him without giving him time to react.

The following movement consists of:

1. Moving the right foot in a semicircle until it reaches behind the opponent.
2. At the same time the arm follows from the left and grabs and raises the opponent's right leg. For the application of the technique we need a safety catch, a bridge that will be our right foot well situated behind the opponent's support foot. It is from here when the application of the foot cut begins with or without previous hook. The direction of this performance will be applied by hooking the foot and directing it to the back (see photo) and as a consequence the opponent will fall over, giving us an advantage and total control once on the floor. The performance also counts on the push of the opponent's foot with the arms.

I don't know if you have realised but all the techniques have been performed going round the opponent from the front to his left, situating ourselves in a radius, sometimes wide sometimes less wide, depending on the techniques that have been applied and culminating with the end of this turning path by taking the final position situating ourselves behind the opponent. Hmmm, this reminds me of Aikido or of Kempo Karate, well, it doesn't matter, it reminds me of many martial arts techniques. Learning what is shown has a little of everything even originality, creation, inventiveness and many years of practice with many broken bones and damaged ligaments, years of life that will not return. Make the most of them, learn the "crème de la crème".

I will let you into a secret, the combinations performed by a circling path, in other words, moving around your opponent while you are applying blows I learnt from the POKEMON series. No, its a joke, they are Judo techniques combined with the rest of the techniques which are shown in the photos.

To be honest, I am not going to tell you all my secrets otherwise they would not continue to be secrets. But in one way or other each student finds his path, some will have enough from everything shown in this and the previous book and I will not reproach them, but the best ones will guess at least a part of what is hidden in each photo, in each explanation, in each word, movement or application.

Don't worry, I was not born like this, I learnt it, so go on learn and feel better today more than yesterday, and better this year more than last year.

You don't understand everything ? You soon will, be patient or have the patience of ZEN, try to win step by step. And the most important thing don't stop following me. I think that you have now read half, how much you have learnt I don't know, but better something than nothing.

COMBINATION Nº 3

Multiple elements, photos: 3.

We will begin with a counter attack defence from the blow that the opponent wishes to apply.
Applied technique, front kick to the abdomen with the left hand already prepared to continue the series of blows or kicks.
Logically the opponent will move back, so what we have to do before applying the blow to the face is to judge the distance, while we are moving, to be able to move the left foot the corresponding distance.

The application of the blow is done at the same time that the foot touches the floor.
We continue to withdraw the left arm and with a small advance we apply the Butt but not before assuring ourselves that our left foot opposes the movement of the opponent's foot.

COMBINATION Nº 4

A couple of simple elements. Four photos plus one. Application of kick behind the opponent's knee together with the preparation of the right hand for the application of the following blow as soon as the opponent moves sufficiently to the front.

Body leans towards the back some 10 degrees.
When putting the right foot on the floor we apply the blow to the face/chin.
The foot stays exactly behind the opponent's left foot.

Application of foot cut by the two corresponding components:

1. The application of the cut at the same time that,
2. The right arm withdraws completing the correct foot cut movement.
Once the foot cut has been applied a mental revision will be carried out of what will follow.

Next we let the opponent's foot follow the direction which we have applied while we put the right foot on the floor.
Once the foot rests on the floor a blow is carried out with the edge of the hand using the necessary rotation towards the left. Our target is the back part of the neck.

In the last photo which is a view from behind the application of the "knife" hand can be observed clearly on the back part of the neck, as the extension of the body from the inside towards the outside giving elasticity and more strength to the blow applied.
Also the effect of the blow can be seen which makes the opponent's body move to the right, looking at the photo.
The left foot is flexed in such a way that the knee makes a straight line with the toes, a vertical line which will be learnt with time. The right foot is in support position with the weight distribution of 60%, and 40% on the left foot.
The rotation has to be done quickly and at the same time with the application of the blow in question.
If you look properly at the position of my left arm in the previous photo, it is in semi bent position which means the preparation of the application of the "knife" blow by the extending of the arm at the moment of performance and rotation.
The blow can also be applied with the fist.

COMBINATION Nº 5

Elementos Simple elements, 3 photos.

We begin the defence by making a Dodge to the left with grab of the attacking element, the leg. Using the right foot to pivot we are going to apply a kick to the back with rotation, to the opponent's kidneys.
As it can be seen in photo nr. two, the left arm makes the opposite movement to the foot which is kicking.
Even in the moment of impact the opponent's leg should still be held tightly.
During the performance the left foot stretches out as much as possible applying more strength or simply applying a short blow followed by a push. Given that we are grabbing the opponent's foot it allows me to apply a foot cut on his support foot, this results is the fall of the opponent, being an easy performance to carry out.

COMBINATION Nº 6 ONE OF THE ONES I LIKE MOST

**Multiple elements,
5 photos.**

Defence against attempt of hand blow to the face. The defence has been done by beginning with the movement towards the opponent in the key moment of his performance. We have applied a blow with movement on top of the attacking arm. Blow and step forward in one action, saves energy. Now that we are well positioned we are going to continue applying techniques and the next one is a foot cut from the back applied to the right foot which is the furthest away. This is to divert attention to a point where we are not going to apply all the strength and neither are we going to continue with it, just the opposite. We will continue with the application of another foot cut thrown by our leg on the back part of the opponent's ankle.

We assure ourselves that the foot cut has applied enough force to the opponent's foot to the front right and we continue. It appears that the opponent has taken the direction indicated by our performance and has brought himself into a suitable position so that we can apply him a very simple but efficient technique, that of the palm blows.

Blows applied with the palm are blows with a pushing tendency but the first thing that they do is make a short contact with the opponent's lungs. Once the double blow of palm has been applied, from a suitable position that assures us sufficient space for blow and push, we prepare ourselves for the application of the following technique DURING the opponent's movement to the front (look at the photo), which is the application of the "cut off air supply" kick to the ribs or even better to the genitals as there is enough space, or the application of the ear cut. If the kick is to the genitals then the position is front and from the back. I want you to understand something which is essential in the performance of the combinations and that is: I NEVER let the applied technique take complete effect, before starting to apply another technique which neither do I allow to finish and I begin again and again applying different techniques.

D. DIRECT TECHNIQUES

The Direct Master Techniques respect the pattern and the description from the first book which is the performance of two movements at the same time. Unlike the first book, in this one advanced techniques are shown with the corresponding explanations. In the photo, application of the technique consisting of blocking with the palm the opponent's fist together with the application of lock to the attacking arm done by our right arm.

How have we got here?
I will tell you; I found myself in combat position and suddenly the person in front of me tried to hit me in the stomach, in this instant I moved to the right totally, enough to be able to apply a diversion of blow with my left palm inwards.
At the same time I performed a lock on him with my right arm and lifted my hand to reach his throat which I could easily get hold of and stay like that until he fainted.
In the second situation almost the same has happened with the difference that this time I have used my palm in another way and position and I have applied a blow to the chin at the same time that the block was being done. This means that I am thinking about applying him another technique.
This time I have situated myself further back.

This time I will not lose more time I am very busy lately.
I haven't got time for games, I will give him the beating he deserves for attacking me and I am in a hurry because I have to get working on the next book.
But look at the block, I have used the palm in a different way, why is that? Well I have to go, you will find out later!

But if I look properly the position is also a little changed and also the body is leaning as if it was being dragged by the arm which is giving the final blow, I don't really know.
It is possible that I tried to give more strength to the blow by pushing the shoulder with the body.
And the lock appears to be applied both on the elbow and the shoulder, in any case it must hurt.
The weight seems to be distributed more on the right foot as if the left was prepared for something.
Another? Please, I'm in a hurry, I will give this big bloke a good blow with the elbow so that it all finishes quickly, there is no possible mistake if you hit him correctly. I like the block with the exterior of the palm, it is to the exterior to create a free field for me towards the opponent's chin, yes I bet that's what its for. I have put my right foot properly, I have almost got the opponent under control, later if I want, I can apply him a knee blow to the "nest", yes, yes I can! And I can even stop playing around with words.

DIRECT TECHNIQUES PERFORMED IN PARTS FOR A BETTER UNDERSTANDING, FOTOS 3.

Ok, in steps. Photo 1, attack started by the opponent towards the medium–high level, straight blow with right hand prepared to apply the second blow. Situation explained.
The first step to take is a firmer and more suitable position in which the spectrum of action can be widened.
The second step consists of grabbing the hand which is applying the blow and twisting it; preparing ourselves in this way for the next step in the performance of a direct technique. My right hand even though it is still hidden is prepared for the application of the blow on the already twisted arm of the opponent. My right foot has also changed place a little preparing the position which has to be taken in the application of the next step of the technique.
The 3rd step is to turn the body in the direction of the opponent's stretched arm and the application of the second lock under the elbow. There exist a multitude of direct techniques with the application of locks and this is one of them but there is not just one type of lock, there are a multitude, very different among themselves, but with the same effect. Next we are going to see some very different ones.

It often happens that things are not explained well in Martial Art classes of any type and I have seen them in various countries and cities. Such as the following considerations: the value of the actions and the importance of “shooting” at the right moment, but in TAUDANC in the majority of cases the right, moment, for example, is considered to be in the 1st second after the opponent has begun his attack. A right moment is also considered, in the majority of cases, to be between the opponent’s actions. Act in the TAUDANC way, while he thinks, while he is about to apply some technique, when he has already begun the attack act immediately with our reply.
One of the advantages of TAUDANC’s way of thinking and reacting is that, once you see the movement of the opponent’s attack, your instinct will apply the corresponding technique, by now you have a clue and apart from this the opponent is busy with his technique application, in attacking.
There are more details that have been explained in the first book but it doesn’t make sense to repeat them.

The performance of the photo has been done in the following order: Finding ourselves in combat position with the right foot forward, the opponent attacks us with a knuckle blow to our abdomen, on practising the advance for the application of his blow the opponent has got closer. At this moment we move to the back enough to be able to avoid the blow, to apply the diversion of the arm with our right arm and the application of the blow with the palm to the opponent's stomach. To be able to understand the movement of the arm that applies the blow with the palm better, one should visualize the position of the same in combat position and from here the continuation described in the photo. If you cannot visualize what we have mentioned, return to the corresponding page and compare both photos. The body leaning a little forward helps the good application of the blow with the palm as is also a great help the slight bending of the right foot so that the hand can have the adequate height for the application of the blow, a type of impact blow. The look, pay attention to my eyes, it is not necessary to look after the blow, act freely.

MORE ...

AND MORE ,

DIRECT TECHNIQUE APPLIED WITH THE FOOT

Side kick used as direct technique.

He has moved first, but I am the one who has hit first.

3. MASTER BLOCK TECHNIQUES

In the 1st photo,

A marvelous double block with movement to the right against a blow that we call the "subidon".

The three movements are done at the same time each one having its function.

While we move to the right, the left palm make a downwards block, time in which a "stop" is applied in the form of a blow with the palm on the opponent's shoulder.

Second photo, first step, the attack with opponent's step. We stretch the arm and we leave space while we are applying a small movement to the front.

With the right foot well positioned the body leans towards the opponent and with the fist formed a lock is applied, the pressure applied of the block is between the arm and our still body.

UPWARDS BLOCK WITH THE PALM

The application begins with both movements at the same time. From the combat position the front foot is used which acts as a support to turn only the sole while, the left foot moves to the back as much as necessary. At the same time the right arm with the open palm applies the diversion of the blow upwards, feet flexed.

The application of the movement to the side has to be taken very seriously while we apply techniques.
The correct taking of the position as well as the correct performance, certitude and stability are essential.

DOWNWARD BLOCK WITH THE PALM

Why have we had to move so far back?
For the simple human reasoning that if the blow tries to reach our head even at the last moment we can avoid it.

Why ?

Because the head has more mobility than the entire body at the time of dodging.
So in blows to the body we have to take precautions of movement.
In the photo, movement to the back together with the twist of the body to the left and the application of the diversion downwards with the palm.

INWARDS BLOCK WITH THE PALM

Scene:
Combat or base position (Open Arms Technique).
Attack with or without opponent's step together with straight blow to the face.
Taking of side position, beginning with the right foot with the body leaning to the back in a perfectly balanced position.
We are not escaping, on the contrary we are putting ourselves in one of the best TAUDANC positions while the body is leaning well and the weight is distributed correctly on the legs.
The recommendable distribution would be 65% on the right foot and 35% on the front one.

VIEW FROM THE BACK

The left arm in specific TAUDANC defence position.
Look at the diversion applied to the opponent's arm.
A photo has been taken from the back to be able to see better: the position of the body, feet, the angle of the arm in application of the block, the angle of the bending of the body totally controlled, in tune with the correct weight distribution on the feet.

The feet are those which lead everything in this application and in others.
It is important to practise until you master this type of essential TAUDANC movement.

BLOCK WITH LOCK

The block TAUDANC style is done with the corresponding movement depending on the opponent's attack.
It is this which imposes the taking of one position or other, of one movement or another or none, but always adapting ourselves to the situation, maintaining the correct characteristics of the techniques.

A light lock has been performed on the attacking arm, the movement was very restricted given that the opponent has not used much strength in his performance.

BLOCK WITH SHOULDER CONTROL

The application of the block whether of the fist or of the shoulder is unique, being like many others found only in the TAUDANC.
In the next book you will see why the shoulder has to be controlled.

The application of the block in question has been done with a movement to the front exactly when the opponent finds himself half way there.
In some way we are giving him what is known as the "welcome".
The body is leaning forward in case it has to be increased.

BLOCK AGAINST SIDE BLOWS AN EXCLUSIVE TAUDANC TECHNIQUE LIKE MANY OTHERS

The application in the photo which is going to be shown next, is a technique that in many disciplines is missed out, almost all of them being focused on direct, front blows. False, in the street you will not be attacked by a student of Karate or other discipline, the majority have no specific preparation and some possess little experience in martial arts. They might think that just because they went to martial arts classes when they were children and have seen some films that they have enough knowledge for street attacks, but its not true.
Yes it is also true that at times it is enough, because the boy, the adult, the citizen who is being attacked is not prepared either, it is not an organized confrontation, nor a championship.

This TAUDANC block, my own elaboration of my street experiences has been created and is aimed at all the blows that come from the side. It can be used as a previous step to this one, the previous photo, even though the performance of the previous photo has another continuation for which other continuation techniques correspond. The movement consists in applying the same movement as the opponent, once here press downwards.

BLOCK WITH THROAT GRAB

Performance:

Movement to the back together with the raising of the left arm, with the application of slight diversion to the outside. At the same time that the left arm begins to rise, the right arm also rises and is placed in a position of grabbing the opponent's throat, therefore also stopping his advance. Ok, we have the hand and the throat controlled. The time has arrived to put the learnt techniques into practice, go ahead, apply what you like, and what best fits, continue as if you were me.

BLOCK PLUS ONE MORE SAFETY ELEMENT

In the picture below against a direct front attack or not, a specific TAUDANC hand block with grab is applied and as the opponent has reached this position we take advantage to create a safety catch for the application in the form of a blow with push, applying it on the back part of the opponent's knee. If you want to increase both techniques you have to squeeze the foot at the same time as our right arm presses to the front and down until achieving good stability.

Block by diversion and lock

Block in two parts:
1. The right hand applies a very fine diversion to the inside while the left hand take charge of grabbing the opponent's fist so that he can later apply a rotation directed downwards and outwards in such a way that the opponent's elbow stays in a light lock, easily controlled. Let's let the opponent get to the distance which he thinks is best for him, but this distance also suits us and furthermore, for the next performance, we are going to get nearer to welcome him.

Continuation

We have applied the second technique.
We find ourselves in a position with our back to the opponent isolating his left arm while the right arm applies a 3rd wrist lock, as it's in a good position, why not?

The body leans downwards to the right as much as necessary to maintain the situation stable. Practically in 99% of situations the opponents recognize defeat.
If the situation threatens, the "joke" kick can be applied to the opponent's stomach or chest at intervals.

BLOCK AGAINST FRONT KICK

Block by grabbing the front kick attack made by the opponent has been done starting from the combat position.
A side movement has been applied in concordance with the existing distance and the distance that we need to find ourselves in a stable position.

This type of blocks with grab are used many times by the opponent as a trick, to get the opponent to approach voluntarily and thoughtlessly. For this reason it should be practised with much speed and always being aware that if you don't do something fast you will be in the reach of your opponent's blows and furthermore, the blows will come from the back. So with both hands that are grabbing the opponent's foot we move a little to the front to distract attention and here with the hand that holds the upper part of the foot and the other that holds the heel we begin to apply the twist of the foot. We are going to begin by strongly directing the right hand and the upper part of the foot towards the right and at the same time the left hand directs the heel in the direction indicated by my right hand but downwards.
I know that practically everyone understands what a twist is and how the arms should move but, hey, I have to explain it for those that have never played in their childhood so that they can learn it now as self defence. Well, I imagine you have got the idea.
If the opponent goes into action, short rotations to the right are made until it is decided which technique should be applied to finish with this situation. And, as we have started, we are going to continue with maximum twist of the ankle.
This way the confrontation will end immediately and once again we have freed ourselves of the aggressor. Although we have the opponent's foot immobile but, it is not the only technique that can be applied in this situation, its just a technique that I wanted to show you, that's all.

Block techniques with the foot and its components

We use anticipated thinking as the main element in the majority of the blocks that are performed with the foot. To know with a fraction of second what is going to happen before it does. In some way at a given time we are all predictable, the question is; what percentage? Can it give the opponent an advantage? Can the opponent make the most of this advantage in a useful time? Another important thing before the performance of techniques is to think that the target is not where it is but some 20-30 cms further back. Practise this habit of mine and you will see the results: more speed and many more advantages that I will let you discover for yourselves by practising. I recommend you start by applying punches and kicks and then follow on with more complicated techniques and combinations that require much mental and physical training. About this photo there is a lot to talk about and we will begin now!

First consideration: That the opponent attacked first, and in defence we apply the front kick with added step approaching and causing with our knee block the lock of the attacking arm.
It is a front kick without the final extension.
Second consideration: That on guessing the technique that the opponent is going to try to apply we have reacted almost at the same time as him. Wow, this is a good one. In both cases the main element is the correct performance of the kick with added step without doing it completely but striking with the knee.
The support foot, once the corresponding movement has been done, has to have absolute control of the balance whether in static position or at the moment of impact with the back part of the opponent's elbow. The hands help the balance and the movement but are also prepared to defend or attack, block, grab etc. In any case if the first time it does not work, turn the body to the right, apply the stoping knee.

Defence against front kick.
Finding ourselves in combat position we let the opponent start his kick. Next a foot blow is applied to the muscle of the attacking foot with our right foot practically in a forward position. The position of the foot at the moment of the application of the blow leans a degree to the left and can be easily observed especially when looking from the knee to the ankle and even the sole.
This blow applied with the foot in such a unique and peculiar position is to protect the genitals and the body while you are striking. The part which draws a line between the distance of the knee and the ankle has contact with the opponent's foot and, due to this contact, creates the control of the opponent's leg and watches to not move the body closer and apply the kick.
The movement of the body is to the back while the direction of the blow is upwards, the blow has to be short and strong.

On the left we have a block done with our foot exactly on his knee, his foot doing a side kick. All effort must be put into carrying out the block exactly on his knee or on the contrary it can be painful for both parts and will look very bad.

Why are these two blocks so special ? I will tell you: because to do them, a special movement has been used. This is similar to the technique called "scissors" in combination with the jump movement towards the front. Previously the opponent's hand has been grabbed.

It is a composition of movements quite difficult to do but everything is possible with practice. They must be practised separately at the start to know weight dispersion properly, to control it and apply the jumped step, always as much as necessary, and amongst other things, such as the breathing, focus and speed.
In the photo below, performance of block with the application of blow with the foot also on the elbow, but any part of the hand that attacks can be hit, on the condition that, it has to be very controlled, strong and rapid, if not the opponent can get hold of your foot.
Attention should be paid to the position of the opponent's arms before the application, their position and tendency to move. In agreement with this, the reaction of our arms should be that of arms tied to his with a long string imitating his movements.

F MASTER PATCH TECHNIQUES

The patch technique consists in catching your opponent by surprise by quickly approaching, sometimes at a distance of between 2-4 meters, sometimes at a distance of less than 2 meters.
Next, follow your opponent's grab, it is the grab that the Bullfighter uses when the bull tries to gore him and he has not had time to defend himself, to leave himself the field free.

But we are going to use it another way and with a totally opposite intention, not allowing the opponent to develop or apply his techniques, we are going to call it "death by trying", (dead in the attempt) which is what he is trying to do.
This is practically the result of the application of the "patch"
The grabs of the "patches" can be different depending on each situation. What I mean is:

What use is a sword to a Samurai in a telephone box?

Well, with this I have said everything about the philosophy of the patch technique, next you yourselves can make your own comparisons such as: Of what use is Karate to someone who is tied up? for example.
As applied techniques, once the opponent is held we are going to number some: beginning by blocking, immobilizing first the arm or foot that was prepared to attack we go on to the diverse techniques that can be applied such as: locks, foot cuts, blow techniques with the elbow, with the knee, immobilization by strangulation etc.
In short, everything learnt that can be applied in a fight at short distance and body to body. The patches are of different types and we are going to show a good part of them.

SIMPLE PATCH

In the photo the execution of a simple patch. Normally with the correct execution of a patch 90% of the opponent's capacity of action is diminished. You can imagine that blows or other techniques will be applied next.

PATCH WITH LOCK

After the rapid approach, a patch with lock has been performed, lock on the throat and the arm which we suppose wanted to apply the blow.
The knee is putting pressure on the opponent's knee giving it more stability and control.
The position always has to be very stable, the lock has to press sufficiently to have control of the situation tightening or loosening depending on what is required in each situation. Squeezing little by little the opponent's left arm, go up, careful he doesn't escape.
The lock on the other side is applied under the shoulder.
Balance is also a very important tool, here it has been used under the concept of a weak lean to the back but also under the control of the knee that tightens on the opponent's knee.
With each centimeter that we go backwards, tighter will the opponent's knee be. The lock has been performed in a simple way, one hand holding the other. In this type of patches and in the majority, attention must be paid to the position of the head so that the opponent does not hit us with his head.

PATCH WITH LOCK 2

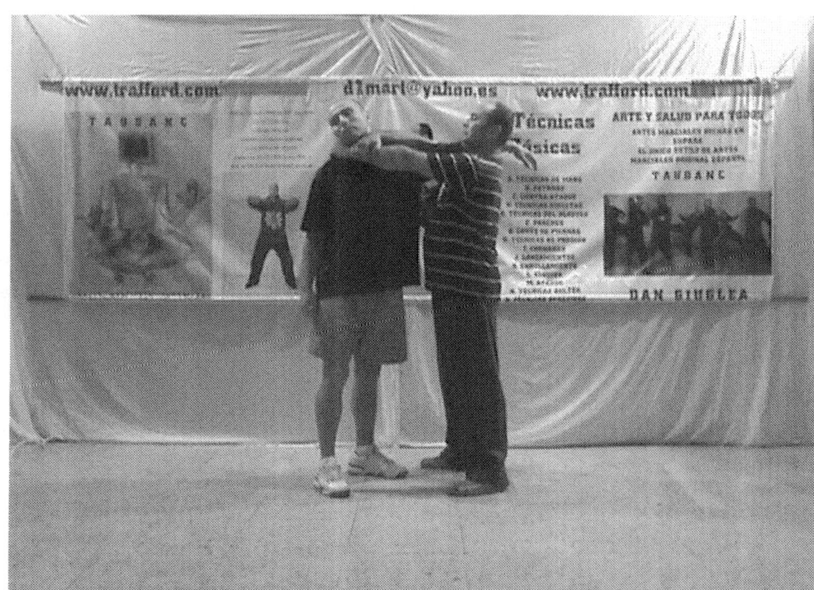

In this type of patches, including the arm of the opponent, the opponent's clothes have been grabbed with one hand and with the other the lock has been closed with a squeeze of the right arm on the left arm of the opponent. Side position.

PATCH WITH LOCK TO THE FOOT

The opponent tries to attack with the right arm which has been well received and directed into the position that we want.
At the same time after the rapid approach a lock has been applied to the opponent's front foot obliging him to bend the foot at our rhythm and still position.
The opponent has a tendency for the body to go forwards, we control his position by the foot which applies the lock.
The left hand has hold of the attacker's arm stuck to my abdomen. The right hand pushes the shoulder to assure the slight lock of the elbow. It must be practised until the perfect point of balance is found and in preparation for the opponent trying to escape or free himself from our lock.
Although this is similar to a previous photo this patch has been done sideways not front ways which supposes a substantial change in the application and distribution of strength and balance whether static or in situations of wich the opponent trying to free himself.

The ideal position has to be found for the application of the knee lock, but the main control is by the tightening or loosening of the arms that with their squeeze can reduce the quantity of breathed air.

PATCHES WITH THROWS TO THE FLOOR

Once the rapid approach has been performed the opponent's legs are grabbed strongly with the arms.
Both movements plus the knocking down is carried out in the shortest time without giving the opponent time to react or defend himself.
The application of the technique consists in grabbing and throwing, bringing down the opponent with the help of the arms together with the push of the shoulder. Everything has to be done with maximum speed and once the technique has been applied without the opponent having the occasion to get hold of us, we continue with the application of a technique of free choice. It should be mentioned that from the first moment that we have made contact with the opponent our shoulder has pushed him, creating an unbalance that provides us the grab and the lifting of the opponent's feet. The only inconvenience in this technique is that if it is not well learnt the opponent will get hold of us, complicating things. Because of this, the first contact done running or in a rapid movement has to be the push of the shoulder followed by one single action: the grab and throw to the floor. Given that the fall can make the opponent hit himself we have to take precautions and in a real situation with the risks and the threat that this person represents for the victim they will be applied or not taking into account the risk.

PATCH WITH THROWS TO THE FLOOR NR. 2

The entrance having been performed, the attacking arm has been immobilized and the opponent's right foot has been grabbed. Our right foot has been put where we believe the centre of the opponent's body weight to be.
The opponent's arm is pulled until we are stuck to it. Don't forget that previously the arm has been immobilized, then a push or shoulder blow has been applied and, finally, the foot has been grabbed, situating ourselves in a calculated, correct position, prepared for the throw of the opponent. We must see the group of elements as one, focusing on the approach and the push which will constitute the diversion of attention for the opponent, then we have to think in the total of contributing elements in this technique and to see it, do it, as one, one single piece, I know that there are a few empty times or mini delays, but try to get the idea and practise and you will see that it is possible.
Passing on to the performance of the throw it works in the following way:

1. Raising and direction of the application together with the change of weight distributed by both participants.
2. The push of the opponent with the right arm to the desired direction.
3. When the right hand pushes, the left pulls and they join on withdrawal.

PATCH WITH LOCK AND GRAB

Considering that the opponent is in a side position, which is the most common, we have approached rapidly and we direct the hand which was in forward position to the back, performing at the same time a permanent wrist lock and through the wrist also an elbow lock.
It is a simple movement to the back, after having caught and squeezed the opponent's hand. From this moment we have him controlled and we can apply the corresponding hold for better stability, good immobilization and good control.
In the second photo a turning movement has been applied until we have arrived at the back of the opponent.
Finding ourselves in this advantageous position we go on to the application of the patch and we begin by grabbing and pulling the opponent's arm to the back, maintaining it immobilized between the arm and the body. The left hand ensures that the arm remains stretched out with the same arm we push, helping the leaning of the opponent, to maintain the arm stretched out.
The only thing left is to grab the foot and maintain the created position.
You can continue to widen the angle of the arm lock and/or the pull of the grabbed foot towards the back. But it all depends on what you want.

PATCH WITH LOCK AND IMMOBILIZATION

Considering that both opponents were in combat position a patch has been applied which is presented in the photo in the following order.
1. Situated in combat position with the left foot forward and the opponent with the arm raised in preparation to apply a direct blow or a blow from above or below, with the left hand the arm is grabbed and held while a jumped step is performed until reaching the position of the photo no two.
2. On getting hold of the opponent's arm, the elbow is passed behind the opponent's elbow in a movement of pull and then twist with the application in the corresponding direction, until we find ourselves in a position of elbow lock of the opponent.
It can be done in separate parts until the times of performances and the gaps are reduced.
3. The foot which contributes to the immobilization has to be positioned in such a way that it has contact with both of the opponent's feet, being capable of acting in an opposite direction to some of the opponent's possible attempts of escaping.
The control of the opponent is divided between the arm which applies the lock and the foot, which makes any movement of the opponent difficult, controlling it. You can continue with various techniques depending on the situation and of our intentions; of immobilization to the floor, of hitting, of complicating the immobilization more etc.
Much practice and study of the technique are necessary for a correct defence and for the application in itself.
The recommended exercises are those which pay much attention to the balance, to the rocking in case of needing to change the technique, of the distribution of weight which can be changeable depending on the movements (if there are any) of the opponent.
It should be practised in slow actions, especially the approaching of the opponent, the lock itself, the transfer of the elbow behind the opponent's elbow and the maintaining of the corresponding position of the lock.

PATCH WITH LOCK OF THE SPINE AND IMMOBILIZATION

After performing the rapid approach, the following movements are applied at the same time: the grab of the foot and the grab of the neck. The grab of both contribute to the extension that must be applied between the leg and the neck. You grab the opponent's chin and you push back in a short movement, controlling only to obtain the immobilization, not to cause damage, believe me it's enough for the moment. The body with both arms situated in position can go back as much as necessary to maintain control. The basis of the performance of the opposite action which contributes to the correct spine lock and to maintain the change of position is our hip. An important factor is the left foot (look at the photo) that can move to the left to increase the curve of the opponent's body or, can diminish maintaining a position of stability. In the same way the right arm (looking at photo) can apply to the opponent's foot necessary force to bend it and aim it to the back in a position of total control. What has to be understood is that these are only examples, each technique having a continuation.

PATCHES WITH STRANGULATION

One of the best applications but the photo should be seen to understand what is important, the photo is only the application of a technique.
In conclusion: a good position is considered correct if it has the components in the places from where a lock and immobilization situation can be created.
We are going to study the photo a little. Basic elements are in this situation: the positioning behind the opponent, the right hand grab of the clothes, the left hand that applies the lock on the opponent's elbow, the application of forced bending of the opponent's left foot downwards creating a controlled tension and the sufficient leaning of our body to the back to maintain the elements in corresponding position.
In the photo below the patch has been applied in a swift way which means that soon another technique is going to be applied. The initial intention is different from that shown in the previous photo which has as its aim a longer duration of the application.
It will not apply any technique next but will wait for the opponent to lose strength, or the application of another technique but after a while.
In the light performance there is always a rapid continuation.

In conclusion: what is a patch? It is just an immobilization in which locks, twists and other techniques are used, but with the aim of immobilizing for a short time or not so short. In the photo, another example of a patch with a lock applied on the spine, the shoulder and possibly on the opponent's foot.

To this, strangulation is added. So we have a patch with multiple locks, strangulation or immobilization. Various techniques can be applied in the application of a patch, but in our examples we only put what is necessary to be able to learn this techniques that are shown in the photos.

Explanations and advanced performances.

You could practically talk for hours about one of the photos or write at least 20 pages or more so that the technique is explained completely; but with what is shown and written, which corresponds to a higher level of knowledge, I consider it as sufficient as efficient. I advise you to study the unseen details in each photo and you will find more details and explanations.

A very special patch with multiple applications, continuations. You have to do what you want with the opponent, make him turn, make him kneel, bend him, hit him etc. He has to be at your entire disposal, for this, you need to begin and then apply techniques.

MASTER PATCH

Ok, let's rewind.

The opponent first attacks with a hand blow, which is intercepted and a wrist lock is applied with the change of position and direction.
Second, continue with a side kick that is intercepted half way.
In this moment our front leg makes, at the same time, a rise towards the outside behind the opponent's foot.
The moment that the left hand grabs the opponent's foot, you continue with the right foot, being an application of a blow inwards with our bent leg, in this way forcing the opponent's foot to stay in the position which we want.
The opponent's foot stays trapped between the left hand and foot and both estimate the stable position that has to be taken, just like the pressure that has to be applied with the foot and the degree of twist of our foot to maintain a stable position.
The control of the opponent is obtained through the control of his wrist and of the immobilized foot.
There is little change in the distribution of weight on the support foot, being helped by the two elements mentioned.
Patch with wrist lock with support on the shoulder and kick to the genitals followed by the placing of the foot on the floor, in the position which suits, depending on the technique that is applied next and of the balance obtained.

G. FOOT CUT

SIDE CUT TO ONE SINGLE LEG

The side foot cut is a very good technique if it is applied at the right moment, that is, always having the suitable distance for its performance and space for the movement applied to the opponent's front foot.
You must distract the attention to be able to approach without danger or it is done by an application of techniques that take us close to the opponent.
With the arms always on guard, we pass to the application of the side cut. The base component in this performance is the shape of the letter V that the ankle forms together with the fingers for the grab and pull to the side of the opponent's foot.
The pull is always applied in front of the support foot and it is always done with the foot forward, the arms take the suitable position always depending on the movement and body balance.
It depends on the performer what strength he wants to apply which is directly related to the desired result.

FOOT CUT FROM BEHIND

The application of the foot/feet cut is applied when fighting at middle or short distance. A distance which many times we have to create ourselves if it does not appear and to apply the technique, if this is what we think best adapts to the situation of real combat. Well, we create the necessary situation by a movement towards the opponent, while the first grab is applied on the forward hand of the opponent, followed by the second grab performed with the right hand on the back of the neck, the clothes, the belt etc .

We have three elements that concur in the presented application. 1.The first grab, 2. The second grab and, 3. The application of the foot/feet cut of the opponent with our foot in a direction from the back towards the front and up. As the arms are raised and directed to the opponent's body, the foot which is in tune with the arms applies the foot cut. All at the same time, so that in the final moment of the performance, as soon as the opponent's body no longer has contact with the floor, the cut is considered done and we pass on to a swift or not swift push of the body following the force of gravity.

It is called with movement because, usually before the performance itself, the opponent is directed to the opposite direction of the real performance, creating an unbalance so as to loosen the resistance of the feet, and apart from this, the technique is applied marvelously while the opponent is moving, moving towards where we direct him.

On moving he possesses less floor contact, with unsure balance, with the distribution of body weight uncontrolled, here is where we take advantage to increase this small unbalance until he no longer makes contact with the floor.

Really, the technique, explained in another way, would be while the arms push or pull the opponent's body in one direction, the foot pushes, raising the opponent's foot or feet in the opposite direction.

The application of the lifting either by the arms or by the foot is essential.

To all this a turning movement can be applied to the opponent, in our case towards the left widening the performance.

OCCASIONAL FOOT CUT OR WITH TRICK

The name denominates both situations in which this so special technique can be applied.
In the photo a trick front kick is applied to which the opponent directs himself (with our agreement) to our foot towards the side with a block.
This is an ideal situation for the application of the typical TAUDANC cut that is used making the most of the attacker's trick or block. With or without grab, the foot cut is applied in both mentioned situations. Situating ourselves on the opponent's side and near to him, with the foot already prepared for performance, we apply a blow pushing to the back of the opponent's leg and to be more precise, exactly behind his knee or some centimeters below. In such a way that he is knocked over or, a very important loss of balance is achieved, giving me an advantage in the application of the following technique, which is of free choice.

The movement must be practised with or without a partner until balance is achieved in the performance and good distribution of body weight. You must get the support foot used to movement.

FOOT CUT WITH HOOK AND THROW TO THE FLOOR

It is called throw to the floor because of the controlled push that our arm applies to the front, contrary to the one that pulls our foot.
The techniques denominated "with fall to the floor" do not imply the application of a push or blow action which leads to the falling down of the opponent, because they are unnecessary.
With respect to the first photo, the starting point is that of combat or base position (arms open).
We move towards the opponent, we grab his front arm and we put our right hand on the back of his neck or back.
Next, one of our feet applies an entrance avoiding the front foot and hooking the foot at the back. We are now in position to perform the foot cut. We pass onto the first application putting the foot hook into action and we give it a direction to the back with a sharp lift. The arms also do their corresponding part, one continues grabbing the opponent's hand until he can be seen to be falling. A moment in which the right arm pushes and the foot pulls in opposite directions and the opponent's arm is freed.

h. MASTER PRESSURE TECHNIQUES

The pressure techniques which will be shown next are different to the basic techniques shown previously in the first book which refer to the basic techniques, to the introduction of the pupil to TAUDANC.

In the photo application of the pressure technique on the collar bone and under the opponent's right chest. The application of the technique does not include the grab of the arm but it is recommended. The technique consists in the correct positioning of the fingers on the points indicated, points on which all the strength available is used in the fingers in a curved shape, like a metallic lock like a bird's claw. The four fingers that squeeze on the upper part are situated exactly behind the collarbone, while the thumb applies the lock with all its force, its intention is to join with the rest of the fingers penetrating the muscle. Of course this is not going to happen, but this is the idea, it is the best way of indicating the path that all the fingers follow at the same time with all the locking force available.
It is recommended not to have the performing arm too bent.

PRESSURE TECHNIQUE WITH ONE SINGLE FINGER

Pressure techniques can be applied with the help of a finger or more than one, a bent finger, the elbow, the fist, the heel of the foot, and other more or less blunt parts of our body. I am trying to show the technique itself and its applications without going into details that, probably, will take me to another book and the creation of a specific academy.

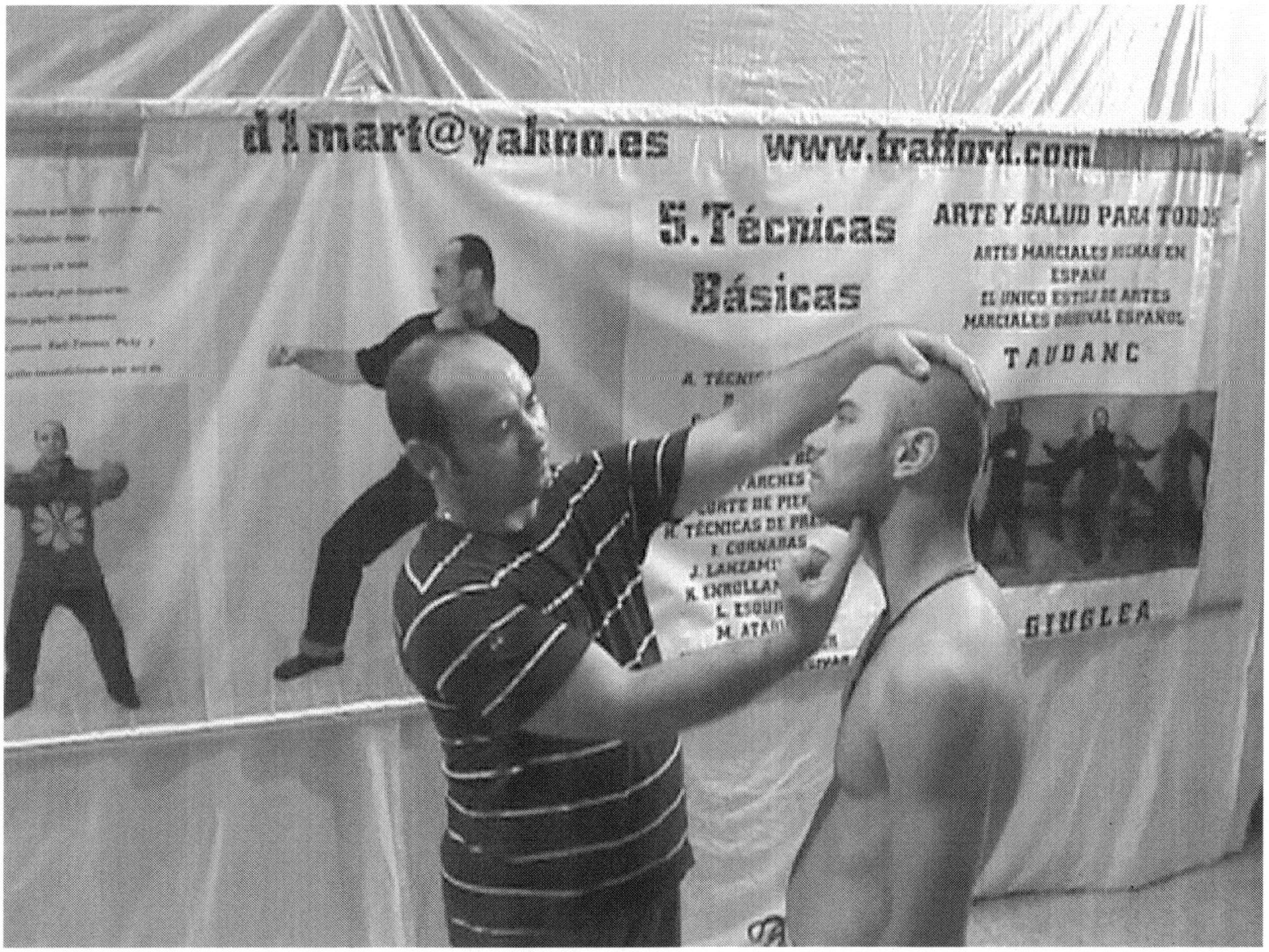

The photo is the demonstration of power of one single finger applying pressure on a sensitive point of the body.
The index finger placed below the jaw begins to push up and inwards or only upwards. For good performance you place the left hand on the attacker's head. The finger can apply pressure or a blow, a finger blow not only under the jaw, but also in many other sensitive points of the body, as for example, behind the ear, the lower part of the neck, on the neck and many other points considered sensitive or nerve centres. Observe and always apply the techniques with the arm only a little bent..

PRESSURE OF ONE OR TWO FINGERS ON THE EYES

A simple study shows us that if the force of pressure from other less sensitive parts is applied on sensitive organs it results in an advantage. At the same time it causes temporary damage to the sensitive organs, whatever they may be, being about two different and opposite persons, one of them is the root of this reaction on the part of the other.

The goal of the application of this technique is the temporary damage that can be caused to the attacker at a short and long distance.
The pressure from the two fingers on the eyes once the hands have practiced the safe and corresponding grab. The fingers have their own degree of twist as in the case of application of the same technique, but as a blow it has a narrower angle and the fingers find themselves in a stable and hard position. Well I have seen many films in which eyes are torn out, but then nobody was judged for it, so apply what is necessary and don't get yourselves into trouble. I can assure you that its enough. You must distinguish when your life is really in danger, to not be so, why exaggerate? Apply just the necessary.

PRESSURE TECHNIQUE APPLIED WITH THE ARMS

Just as we have said, the application of the force of pressure can be applied on various parts of the body denominated as sensitive parts or nerve centres. In the picture we have the application of a force of pressure on the opponent's ankle using the arms.
The application of a key (lock) is used to maintain the opponent's foot in a stable position without moving too much or falling.
Beginning from the combat position with the right foot forward, the opponent begins his attack with a front kick at medium level.
We react by applying a dodge technique with half rotation towards the right, a moment in which we hold the opponent's foot and follow with the application of the pressure technique. It is one of the multiple techniques that can be and at times ought to be combined for the performance of another that needs to be applied in a given moment, imposed by the combat situation. Observe the stable position needed, with the distribution of weight in such a way that contributes to a firm stability. The technique has a disadvantage, the back remains uncovered, but everything has a solution, solve it.

I. BUTTS

Butts, basically, are applied using; the shoulder, the back, the head. Next we are going to demonstrate and explain this very Spanish technique. I can still remember the times when I was studying the movements of the bull, its focus, the moment chosen for action together with other components. Later came the practice, the rehearsals,...and here we are, reading about it.

BUTT WITH THE SHOULDER AT HIGH AND LOW LEVEL

Butts can be performed with or without movement towards the opponent. Butts are push techniques, sometimes done in a form of mass block and blow at the same time, with the corresponding rotation. It is the push that the bull applies in its defenses or attacks; we are going to use it in the same way as the bull.
The application of the thrust implies a certain degree of turn which is determined by many factors, but the main one of influence is the attacking one.
In photo nr. one it is applied in defence without movement, but with the lean and necessary and corresponding strength to the impact.
In the second photo we also see a defence with the application of the butt to the hip or under it.
In both photos, but especially in the first, the correct position of the right foot can be seen situated to the side or behind the attacker's left foot.

BUTT WITH THE BACK, HIGH AND LOW LEVEL

Ok, we are going to turn our backs.
Unlike the butt with the shoulder, this technique has a special characteristic, the curvature of the back used as a tool of blow, block, defence or attack. Practice is essential to be able to learn the correct application at the right moment, get used to curving the back at the precise time anticipating the impact, preparing yourself for the moment of impact. The turn which the body makes is a factor of much responsibility in the movement and placement of the feet as is also the correct flexion of the same. The bend of the body, be careful with the bending, the result of the impact also depends on it. We do not move backwards, he falls or moves back. This has all to be contemplated like the application of a blow using a special tool. It is recommended that the position of the feet be that which is shown in the photos, for the simple reason that it offers the best balance and resistance to the impact. Being about a zone with much point of impact you must think that the attacker will feel the reaction like crashing against a brick wall or against the bull itself. It is not a technique of little strength, on the contrary, put all your strength without positioning yourself too much to the back, just the necessary, always the necessary, don't lose your balance, butt.

BUTT WITH THE HEAD, HIGH AND LOW LEVEL

**Now we are going to be like the bull.
The first thing that I advise you to do is to check the power of this technique. It is done with the clear application of the blow towards the front with strength, as in the photos.
The back has to be curved in a way that offers all the resistance; the head, the neck and the spine transform into one invisible tool.
So, when you are going to apply the technique, think about this in all your trainings or confrontations.
In the photo, a movement is applied towards the right to be able to avoid and grab the attacker's foot and then the butt is applied directly to the opponent's chest.
The application of the blow can be direct to the front or with the head down, in this case the direction and the strength transmitted would be forwards–down.
Very important, this technique is applied with much strength of blow and has the character of an attack, even though it isn't. The blow has to be strong, the feet support the necessary movement and they adapt to the movement, preparing themselves for the impact. You do not withdraw one centimeter in this technique, the effect is total, positive. There is no other option, it has been proved. The risk is presented when you go further than necessary and apply the blow with little strength. Therefore calculate the distance well.**

J. MASTER THROWS

These are techniques of grab and throw. Usually they are used as a counter attack, they are applied in defence, against blows and kicks. They work similarly to the foot cut techniques, that is, as one body part pulls, another helps by pushing in the same direction, or in the opposite one. In throws, as you throw the held element, the hip lifts and pushes helping to achieve the application of the technique. This is the general description, but we are going to see techniques in which the back is not used, we are going to use other movements entirely, using and directing the opponent's strength.

The same path is used, the direction already been given to its extremities by the attacker, we are only going to participate in this action by increasing and directing.

Throws can be with or without foot cuts, after an applied block, front or sideways as a starting or end direction.
They can be applied with movement towards the opponent at the moment that he begins his attack, without letting him continue, and from here, we continue, we take control.
They can also be done without movement or with movement in defence towards the back.
Turns are an important element which are applied in some techniques whether it be the catching of the attacker's arm or foot, respecting its direction of application and increasing it in our way and for the purpose that we had previously decided in the hours of training, here we only apply the performance of a learnt practice and the application of the same or other.

They are used much, the turns, the spins, lowering of levels, radical distribution of the distribution of the body weight. It is very much like the Roll technique because of its nearness to the opponent, in some cases sticking to his back or a different part.
The throws and projections can be single or combined with other elements, but always using the strength and direction of the attacking element, even though at times it is necessary to modify this initial path by turns, rotations, pushes or other elements that are considered adequate to be combined with the basic throw technique.
The aim of the throw is to fling the attacker with a projection using various directions, but almost always using the direction of the strength and the technique begun by the attacker.

The performance can be from very near to the opponent which means carrying out an approach, if not the attacker will provide it, we help ourselves to create a necessary distance for the performance of some techniques.
But everything must adapt itself to the real combat situation, always.

THROW WITH FALL OF LEVEL

We begin by getting hold of the attacker's hand by the wrist. In one single movement we aim our arm to the outside and with a turn of the arm upwards from the inside.

To this we add the fall of the level, the taking of position is that of the photo. At the same time, the arm is pulled forwards. The three movements happen at the same time. The hip and the right foot make a wall to be able to block the opponent's right foot, if necessary.

Next the throw is applied in which, if necessary, the other arm is used to increase the force of the throw to the inside in an inwards circular path. The body weight plays an important part by being the main driving force of all the action that will be followed by the rest of the elements, performed at the same time.

In the photo on the right, the opponent has avoided a fall, even so, the side kick which follows is his.

THROW WITH TURN

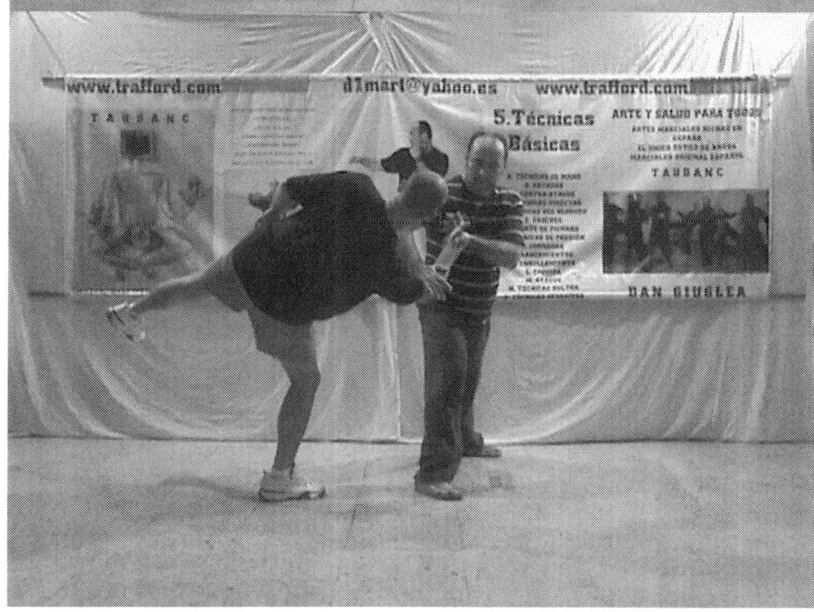

Performance:
Grab of the opponent's wrist, placing of the right hand on the inside part of the elbow and in one single action:
1.The turning movement to the back moving the left foot.
2.The application of force with the palm until the attacker's arm bends just the necessary to be able to be easily controlled with our arms, directing him like this and forcing him to follow our movement of rotation. And this rotation can be increased together with the push on the attacker's arm downwards.

If the parts are respected and the order of performance which describes them, there is no need to increase the turning movement to the back, together with the application of more strength on the bent arm of the attacker. The performance is simple and the opponent falls in an instant without realizing what is happening. But you have to be quick, to apply the hold of the wrist, to know how to handle it in the necessary direction, and to bring it to the final position to end the application in twist position or not, but following the applied path and driven by the action made up of all the elements, that are integral parts in this performance. The idea is that, these elements with practice, transform into one, but for the time being it is enough to take it all in to be able to apply the technique correctly.
It must be understood in parts and then apply the whole.
Use your body weight to direct the attacker, create unbalance.

Throw with double grab

Attack of the opponent from the combat position with the left hand in position. A position which we are going to use to place our arm under and bit by bit begin to push, first forwards and then, following the rotating movement of the body, begin with the left foot to the back until we reach the position of photo nr. two. Principally, the left hand applies a block on the opponent's attack, but as the process of the application advances, the palm holds the opponent's right forearm and the right arm begins to push from below the opponent's elbow to the front upwards and to the left, the left hand pulls to the front and down.

Both movements follow the body turn. The throw can be applied to the side, to the front, to the direction considered suitable with the corresponding rotation. Only by continuing applying rotations does the attacker fall.

THROW WITH ACTION ON THE NECK

Action:
Application of block by light diversion, application of blow to the neck followed by the grab of the same. Preparation of the performance of the body turn to the back, moving the left foot, grab of the opponent's left arm, application of strength and necessary impulse to the body turn, that directs all the elements of the mechanism adequate for this performance. If you don't understand it I will tell you that the turning movement is that which is used in other Taudanc techniques with a small difference, in throws, the turn is wide and can be widened more. The throw can be to one side like in the photo, it can be to the back and if we want it to transform into a final blow, we apply a foot cut, with our right foot on his right foot, and that's it, finished, end of the defence.
Look at my palm. No more comments.

THROW IN 3 STEPS, 3 ACTIONS

First photo: starting position of the technique with step towards the back, right foot, hands and feet prepared to continue the direction of the attacker's arm.

Photo nº 2, we are in position with the hand grab on top and the left foot in front, forward. At this moment we position ourselves properly so that we can follow with the application of the technique. The arm well held and both our arms extended.

Photo nº 3, turn to the left until getting almost in front of the opponent.

The left hand maneuvers the opponent's wrist and lifts it in a twist, preparing it for the next step.

The right arm comes to help the left arm and applies a grab with pressure on the already bent wrist of the attacker.

Finally, the necessary pressure is applied on the bent wrist with both palms, in an up down direction together with the movement of the right foot inwards, towards the opponent. The three movements at the same time; press and turn.

THROW WITH GRAB AND PUSH

Diversion with side step to the back, and neck grab and then grab of the attacking arm. As we change position, the push of the hand that was attacking is applied together with the left hand which pushes and directs the neck.
The push can also be applied on the back. It is simply a change of positions done in the application of the pushes mentioned.
Do not let the opponent free until he is moving.

THROW IN DEFENCE WITH GRAB, FOOT CUTS, SHOULDER AND ELBOW BLOCK

In this defence action, we have as an advantage the excessive movement of the opponent in his attack.
We only make the most of the approaching.
A rotation is done to the right at the same time that the neck and hand of the opponent are grabbed.
The attacker's hand, in the moment prior to lifting his body with our hip, is in a elbow lock, created by the forced stretching of the arm provoked by our left hand, and on our chest.
The shoulder is also in a lock situation being situated on top of our ribs or some part of the back side.
The right hand maintains the position which soon will move to the front with the application of the foot cut maintaining the strangulation of the attacker's neck.

Do you sometimes feel trapped or defenceless?
Well this should be the feeling, you can't move and you are being thrown in a not yet known direction and to increase the worry, suddenly contact with the floor disappears.
So as not cause maximum damage, the hand that strangulates the neck sticks to the chest, while both of the opponent's feet are cut, movement applied together with the lifting of the opponent and the throw.

FRONT THROW AND SIDE THROW WITH INTERCHANGE OF POSITIONS

The technique is applied beginning with a movement towards the opponent a little after he begins his attack, in our case with the right hand.
Three movements at the same time:
move to the attacker, grab the hand which is attacking and, direct it to a free space that allows us to advance.
The application of the blow to the throat is with the edge of the hand or the arm. The movement is to the front a little to the left side to create space. The body leans to the front, the grabbed arm goes back being directed with our left hand as much as possible and well held. The arm which applies the blow is transmitting the strength generated by the movements of the body, of the waist and of the shoulder by the leaning of the body as described. In the second photo we have a performance with interchange of positions, that is, from the present position we occupy the place of the attacker, while, with the application of a push and the action of pulling and directing that our arm performs the action is complete.
The points of application and direction of strength are on the opponent's arm and neck, led and directed by the turning body movement and the strength which is applied. They can be performed separately or together.
Photo one and two.

K. MASTER ROLLS

For those who wish to roll with their opponent or attacker. I offer you some ideas of performance.
But first I will describe the technique. It is the technique of stopping blows or kicks without altering the direction of them and to counter attack in the opposite direction, or to apply one of the TAUDANC techniques by following the direction of the attacker's blow, making the most of his loss of balance. Follow his blows at the same time that you are applying a diversion, a grab, an approach movement, until finding yourself in a situation stuck to him.
Next we are going to show some applications of the technique used against kicks.

Defence against side kick.

By a movement to the right side the field is left free for the foot which applies the kick, while with the turning movement the opponent's foot is grabbed. In the second phase, almost all the body weight is left on the leg, taking the corresponding position.
You can continue to apply a lowering of level by reaching with the grabbed foot half a step more forward and lowering, in such a way that the final position will be with the feet flexed, especially the right one and the position of the opponent's foot is between the foot and under the arm.

The technique has as its objective the foot lock, a lock applied on the knee. At the same time, to control the situation a movement is applied to the front creating a situation of relative immobility and limitation of the attacker's movement.
If we want to break his leg we pull more to the front in the sitting position without loosening the foot grip.
But there are other possibilities of fighting such as, for example, from the position shown in the second photo.

After applying the lock you may continue to take an opposite position to the one shown and with a turning rotation towards the right, applying the necessary force so that the opponent follows our movement.
Once this has been achieved, you let the opponent fall freely, continuing the off balancing and the direction which we give to this application. Another possibility is that of the application of a foot cut of the opponent's support foot with our right foot, after applying the lock. Also after the lock, part of the opponent's foot can be turned, and I refer to the inside part, from the knee to the heel on which a forced twist of the leg is applied.
To this action a turning rotation is added to the left, until we are able to rest our back on the upper muscle of the opponent's foot, applying all the body weight.

We let ourselves fall with the grabbed foot onto the opponent's foot or his hip. One of the most simple and most used applications, but not the best, is the application of the kick backwards against the abdomen or genitals, after the lock. The forward movement covers our back, while the opponent is obliged to follow in a situation of impotence in his reaction. Also it makes him increase the opening of the feet, which causes him upset. He is aware that he is at a disadvantage, but he does not have time for reaction, the grab annoys him, but he has no choice than to follow the directions which we indicate.

Bend your body, depending on the situation, the bending of the body has to transmit all the necessary body weight without losing balance. The student has to be capable of changing position by turns and application of the lock, changing position as many times as he wants until he decides to change technique.
Maintain the attacker controlled, don't let him take the initiative, don't loosen the grip and neither should you decrease the weight applied on the opponent's foot or body.
Maintain the components even if you have to turn or change position. If the applied technique seems to be the suitable one for this attacker it may be continued until the opponent falls over and we fall on top of him. We provoke the fall without stopping the control of the held foot, the weight and the position of the fall, which has to maintain the obtained advantages. The fall does not imply the freeing of the other one's foot, you may continue applying locks.

DEFENCE AGAINST FRONT KICK

What we do in the majority of cases is practically roll the attacking element.
With the left hand first, the knee is blocked, followed immediately by the grab of the heel with the right hand and is maintained in this position.
The position of the body adopts the optimum position to take the next step in the application of this technique in this situation.
Next a semi turn is made to the right until reaching the position shown in the photo nº 2.
The turning movement finished, all the available strength is applied (70 or 80%) for the foot lock.
Our left arm has the opponent's leg stuck to our body.
The movement is started by the right foot followed by the body and its direction is to the front to increase the opening of the opponent's feets. From this position various techniques of continuation can be applied such as : push with our hip on the side of the knee, turn of the body to the left, application of an elbow blow, the application of a foot cut on the opponent's support foot to the back or to the front. As in the photo, apply a withdrawal to the back by a rotation to the right followed by putting the opponent's foot on the floor pressing with all our weight on the held foot.
As it is not possible to explain everything, I believe that what is written is sufficient and efficient.
However there is more.

L. MASTER DODGES

There are two types of dodges: one which uses block elements and those described and shown in this chapter. The difference between the two is obvious, in the master dodges the Dodge technique is used exclusively, we are not going to block, we are not going to grab, and we are not going to push. We only have to let the blow be consumed without touching the target. It is a game that has to be learnt.
The opponent cannot touch you, it is forbidden, and for this you need to use rapid movements, at the same time that you assure yourself the necessary balance for the performance of any technique, block, attack, thrust, foot cut etc. We are going to see three essential examples to get the idea of dodging. In photo nº 1 it doesn't matter in which position we begin, we have to reach this position to avoid a front blow.

How ?
By giving a step to the side, and I advise you to give the side step situated nearer to the opponent and the attacking arm, not towards the other side.
Let's get into situation; here we have close to us the opponent's stretched hand and his body, thing that confer us great advantage. The possibility of applying techniques by being close to the opponent and most importantly, in a moment in which the opponent and his mind are occupied with the performance of his technique, the front blow. The side step is only a side step and is towards the opponent. You must design your own advantages using anything, an opponent's performance, a chair that is to the side also is good, not to hit him on the head with but, for example, to put it in his path, in his attempt to get nearer. And don't do it with the hands, but use the feet and put it where you want, without hurting yourself. As you are seeing, the factor "contemplation" and mental study of the opponent has a primordial character. In TAUDANC it is not about kicking but understanding why, when, how and with direct reference to "causes and effect". A complete analysis of the situation and of the related elements is recommended. What can be done with a minimum spending of energy.

The game is very easy: don't let him touch you, but don't get too far away so as not to lose the advantage of the closeness, avoid blows but take positions that can be used un your blocks, attacks, or other techniques. The technique is useful whether in closed spaces or in open spaces.

If you master this technique you gain at least 15% strength, dispersed by the attacker who is trying to reach you.
Also you get an idea of his technique, his strength, and his movements. But you have to be quick, quick in thought and this can be done easily. DO NOT THINK, ACT, let your instincts act freely. Do not think about what you are going to do and neither about when or how, don't let yourself be touched and when you consider that it is the time to respond then do it.

Practise the elasticity and balance that you need in the different movements that you are going to apply, movements that neither you nor I know, so practise imagining opponents.
In the photo below, a very wide rotation belonging to the technique is applied. Starting from combat position, facing the attacker, the rotation is begun by moving the right foot situated at the back, in combat position, to front, until it reaches the side of the opponent.

It is a very advanced dodge technique, and very well practised because of its high degree of difficulty, but marked by all the advantages that these positions can offer. The attacker advances to the front.

M. MASTER ATTACKS

**I am going to classify the attacks in two parts:
Natural attacks and Trick attacks.
Next shown are some chosen examples in agreement with the level of preparation and in this book they are called master techniques.**

Let's get to the action. Grab, step forward, and blow to the chin. When I say blow, it means that my "elastic hand" makes it possible to disconcert the opponent. Maximum speed, supersonic! Each photo shows the application of a technique. They can be performed separately or together. Going back to the first photo, the opponent is still not ready for defence so, if we have the intention to follow with the techniques that are shown next, we are going to do it out of habit, not because of necessity. Ok, lets continue with the second photo. Application of kick with the sole of the foot with a speed never seen before, until the opponent's knee almost touches the floor. The movement begins at the hip. The third photo, application of butt.

The application of the butt is made with added step increasing in this way the body strength that was already used. Imagine a bowling ball crashing into a rubber doll, this should be the provoked effect, the opponent's arm can now not be seen, we move it to the back ,making space for ourselves, towards the point of impact.

The eye, the eye is very important, it tells you the deepness, the size, the color, functional images of the brain.

Subconsciously basing yourself on this information, act.

Through the eye, sensations are experimented which oblige you to move one way or the other, the eye studies, collects details.

The eye sees, the brain interprets and the data base dictates what you have to do, therefore, try to overtake this point calculated and imposed by I don't know who, and integrate it into the human functions, and act freely. Your self consciousness has to be increased, only man can observe himself and be aware. Life is little more than a vegetative state.

Be aware of what has been said till now and, in all your confrontations, in all your studies and actions, it is TAUDANC.

In this life it is all about physics and chemistry nothing else, but that is also just a saying, as many of the others that we have expressed in this book and the first, they are only sayings, until when?

Until they stop being so. Another important point is the mood.

The mood has to be adapted, accustomed, educated to take the necessary form at the moment when it is needed to fight.

Ok, enough of philosophy, neurology and other brain sciences.

Returning to the photos and beginning with the first, the "elastic hand" technique has to be applied as quickly as you can. The direction at the start is straight, but after the impact it is directed downwards, which makes the blow harder and provokes disorientation, even in the brain that now does not know where to direct the head as a reaction from the received blow. In the second photo, the blow is applied from the back to the front and down, it is not a push, it is a powerful blow, it hits. In the third photo, make yourself space and with the added step transmit all your strength through the shoulder.

The position taken after the movement indicates the applied strength and increase of your opponent's movement.

The closer you are to your opponent, more powerful will be the effect of the application of the butt.

But take into account that there is a limit to the distance of performance, don't close yourself in completely, if you do not want to find yourself in the situation of the samurai with his sword in a telephone box. I know that you have to pay attention to everything and act in consequence but, how much time will you need to react?

Try it and see and if you are not satisfied, look for a solution to reduce this time.

Try and anticipate your opponent's movements.

Composition of the attack separately and together

The principal element in these performances is the side step to the front until we are situated behind the opponent, applying side step with jump or skip. The mentioned movement has the shape of “<”.
The lower part corresponds to the first side-front movement and the second describes the getting closer to the opponent.
The beginning of the movement is started by the front foot.
Avoiding the attack, we apply a blow from the back.
We can continue or not, with another blow with jump, from up-downwards on the area situated between the throat and collarbone of the opponent.
The left hand grabs and keeps the opponent in position, as much as possible, in this way controlling his movements.

Other 2 Examples of Natural Attacks

Direct front blow to the nose. The distance between the opponent's arm and foot at the moment of impact is mentally calculated beforehand, that which is considered ideal, and without risk, the movement and blow are applied.
A light attack, a natural one with components that use little energy, but of great impact. Special care must be taken on applying the movement, not to trip over the opponent's foot.
The left arm in rearguard ready for action. Lean the body on front foot forwards to give strength to the fist at the moment of impact.

An Exceptional Natural Attack

It is one of the performances that I most like for its quick and exquisite, as well as simple, performance. Grab of the front arm and application of the side kick. The impact is so well calculated that in the majority of cases just with this attack well applied the fight ends, leaving the opponent out of breath.
The secret consists in the application of the kick once the grab has been applied, pulling the arm so that the opponent reacts with an opposite action, which makes his body, while trying to escape, into a immobile target. Forcing his front foot to stretch out and,
Bang, you hit him.

NATURAL FORMED ATTACK

Application of blow with the knuckles, taking the suitable and preparative position for the following application, the side kick. Application of the blow once the foot which is moved touches the floor, the right foot prepares for the application. The body must be ready for the share of balance and strength in the directions which are going to be used. Movement of the foot always trowgh back. On applying the blow with the knuckles, the opponent goes back sufficiently to be able to attain the necessary space and we apply the side kick.
The movement together with the contrary movement of the left arm and the position of the left arm on guard.
Taking this position with the left arm is not only so that it can be used in following applications, it also contributes to the impact.

OTHER EXAMPLE OF FORMED NATURAL ATTACK

Actions which can be performed separately. Block by slight diversion, the getting close of the left foot and application of blow to the chin. Followed, if you wish, by the grab of the opponent's hand, pull to the right and application of the second blow from behind to the back of the neck. The components of this performance depend on and are directed by the good correlation between the movement which makes us finish behind the opponent and the correct following of the arm which is grabbing. The arm which grabs, throws at the right moment and corresponds to the foot stability when taking the new position for the application of the blow to the back of the neck.

The position taken orientated to the right confers us a field full of possibilities of application of multiple techniques.

ATTACK WITH TRICK Nº I

I am going to give you a surprise. Whoever is looking at the photos will say, so what?, I already know that!
Really?
Explanation:
Simulation of attack with front kick, the body prepared for the next step.
The hands help the balance of the body in the next action and soon you will understand what I am talking about. In the second photo the "joke" kick to the head is applied, not the kick called by some "despacho", or called by others circular or roundhouse kick.
So for its performance specific balance is needed given the singular movement of the foot. In the application of the circular kick, for example, the foot, after tricking, is withdrawn and then is deployed to kick the opponent's head.
What we do here is nothing like the previous description.
The real movement is driven by the rotation of the body to the left, taking the necessary balance, at the same time that the foot follows the same movement and finally strikes with the side of the ankle and sole.

Much time is gained because, in my technique, the foot does not need to be withdrawn and then deployed.
It is a natural, efficient movement, why complicate it?

ATTACK WITH TRICK nº2

Again trick with the simulation of front kick application, this time as a second action we have the application of front kick to the face, a special front kick.
Before passing to the second part we have to test and assure our balance.
The kick in question is a front kick to the face, but performed in a different way, for which we need extra balance and the corresponding rocking to the back.
The movement begins from the position shown in the previous photo, the foot going in an upwards path, semi bent, raised to the level of the opponent's face.
The following part consists in the stretch of the foot by some 15 centimeters, touching the opponent's face or chin.
This is followed by a downwards push, which is the last part in this action having to be done carefully, because there is a risk of getting caught in the opponent's clothes, it has been proved.
If the corresponding push is applied and the technique is applied as it should be, there is no risk.

Look at the support foot and think that what you have to do is to assure the balance and the body rocking which assures you the lifting of the support foot.

ATTACK WITH TRICK Nº 3

The trick consists of the simulation of the blow to the face. In effect, we are going to apply a kick. The stretching of our arm occurs at the same time as the lifting of the foot which applies the kick. If he tries to block my foot I hit him in the face with my fist, but let's continue. It is a double edged attack, but the question is: are you prepared for the performance of both techniques, of one or the other depending on the opponent's reflexes? It is easy to say yes, say it, it doesn't cost anything, but to be prepared for what we say does cost something, hours of study, rehearsals and preparation. Returning to our sheep, the technique applies a trick with the hand while a circular kick directed to the opponent's ribs is applied. The technique can be perfected by adding the grab of the opponent's hand, pulling it to the back and transforming it into a stable lock. Contributing stability, if necessary, even for our newly created balance, adding a new element.

Always when an element is added or removed, the balance has to take on its new form, stable and mobile. Apply the body rocking in complete harmony with the deploy of the foot and the impact.

N. MASTER BULTER TECHNIQUES

Next some demonstrations of Bulter techniques. Bulter techniques are obtained from the imitation of those applied by the dog known as a English Bull Terrier and they refer to the application of techniques on one single element at a time; only on the opponent's arm, the leg, body etc. It is the technique of grabbing and not letting go until the element in question cannot be used, at least for a time, by the attacker. It was presented in the first book and we continue now.

BULTER TECHNIQUE APPLIED ON THE ARM

The example consists of three blows applied to the attacker's arm. The first may have a block characteristic, but it is not necessary, it can be applied while the attacker finds himself in combat or waiting position. Talking about the first blow, we can affirm that it is applied exactly on the upper part of the elbow with a coefficient of 100% strength and at maximum speed. It is a blow with the knuckles, but applied with the wrist or forearm. The left hand gets ready for the application of the second blow which is directed to the forearm between the wrist and the elbow, the same strength of 100% is applied at full speed and one after another. The right hand withdraws rapidly and prepares for the next blow, taking the necessary distance for the future application on the same arm.

In the last performance we showed how to grab and bend the wrist before applying the final blow. With the twist of the wrist we obtain the keeping still of the arm and the contraction of its muscle so that at the moment of the application of the blow it has more effect. Pay attention to the three positions of my body in each

one of the performances. The first begins with a rotation towards the arm on which the Bulter technique is going to be applied and while we apply it, the position is always being modified looking for the preparatory balance, for the next application. There is also a bending of the body that you must make in each performance, a bend which confers more balance while you are choosing the optimum distance for the application of techniques.

The final blow in the series is a "hammer" blow applied to the elbow. The elbow finds itself in an impossible and unnatural position so that a blow produces a lock or the impossibility of using the arm. You can continue with more techniques which we can apply on the same arm, but we consider that, with the three applications well performed, we have applied the technique correctly and the result does not stop showing the effect of our application of BULTER techniques. Have you noticed the interchange of hands, as one is hitting, the other is already preparing for the next movement. Together with this, the interchanging of positions (it has to be understood that in reality this interchange of the position of the hands has no effect on the stability or strength) without movement, the bend and the correct position of the feet corresponding to each short or reduced rotation and the adequate use of the spine and the shoulders.

Everything has to work the same way, at the same time, because if the opposite happened they would appear to be separate elements, movements without strength and certainty, something neither here nor there, done just for the sake of it, without effect and lacking importance without impressing the opponent.

I advise you to practise the union of the described elements and to use them as one in your application of techniques.

Bulter Technique Applied on the Leg

Composition of three blows. The first (right photo), consists in the grabbing of the foot with the left hand and the application of the first blow to the thigh. Our position must be with the feet slightly bent, the body bent a little to the left, to the back.

Spreading of body weight on the feet by 50/ 50%. The abdomen hardened ready to receive the blow, the blow which is weak, being interrupted by the action of our arms. Back slightly curved, used strength 100%. Here the relationship can be seen and clearly understood: feet-line of the back, and finally the forearm, which maintains a position of iron, applies the blow. Nobody can touch me, I am prepared and I have the necessary tools in position.

That is the idea, learn it.

The second photo shows us the application of the second blow, the change of one body position to another, from where the strength proceeds, where the strength is transmitted, the point of application: amazing. Look and learn the movement comparing the positions of both photos. I have to mention that the point of application has to be very precise, if not it will be a failure giving the opponent the possibility of counter attacking.

The blow is applied to the side of the knee, which by nature cannot move. The blow is applied by our forearm, but not before applying the necessary rotation for the application of strength, impacting with an area of the arm where the muscle has the maximum resistance and firmness. I suggest that you practise the movements only until you are able to control them and then add the rest of the elements of this technique to your applications.

The practice of the movements separately gives good results, because once accustomed to the specific TAUDANC movements, you realize that they are or can be used also in other techniques. They are indispensable and are directly related to each technique and in many cases, related to various ones.

Photo nº 3. Change of position and application of ankle lock.

The hands grab the outer parts of the foot, one grabs the upper (the toes) the other the heel and a downwards rotation is applied. It begins with the right hand which pushes downwards, while the other hand rises, creating a semi circle of the foot's rotation. Both actions are at the same time.

If you look closely, the application of the rotation is exactly in the opposite direction towards the position of the application of the blow on the knee. The pressure is still maintained on the previously hit knee.

If a turning movement towards the right is applied or an approach, it puts the opponent in an even more difficult situation. The bending of the body gives the situation control and assures stability.

The first blow is applied on the ribs on the right hand side of the opponent. The blow is done with the application of the added step and by lowering the level, under his hand which is situated on guard. The body bends towards the front together with the adequate flexing of the feet. The body weight is spread on both feet by 50%. Observe the position of the shoulders, the right shoulder is not situated in a forwards position, which denotes strength in a compact way, the left arm is in rearguard.

The application of this blow, in its actual position, also has another explanation. It is performed in this complex way because we want, apart from hitting, to control with our forearm, situated underneath, any movement of the opponent's arm.

The angle of the arm can be observed, it is not extended completely. Why?

Look at the first photos in the book and you will see that it is a master technique with the arm situated under the opponent's arm; a possible attack can be diverted, only with the application of the extending of our arm in an upwards direction.

Next, in the previous photo a movement around the opponent is made towards the left, situating ourselves behind him. From this position the second blow is applied to him directed at the kidneys. The position of the performance is firm and straight with the right arm which withdraws at the moment

of the application of the blow.
With the withdrawal movement, strength is applied to the fist which is hitting, helped by the shoulders and the back with movement towards the left.
From the present position, we pass to the next position, corresponding to the technique which is going to be applied. That of hitting the same place with the forearm.
The driving force of the technique, together with the rest of the components, is the movement of the body weight, which before was distributed in an equal way, to its redistribution in a percentage of 65% on the semi bent left foot and 35% on the foot which stays at the back, the right one.
The bent of the moving body also drives and transmits the movement of the arm as well as increasing the applied strength.
We prepare the back foot for the next movement with change of situation.

Through the movement of the soles to the right, the corresponding position is taken in the application of the present blow, side elbow blow on the ribs of the left hand side of the opponent.
The distribution of the body weight is the opposite to the one before, 65% on the front foot, which in this case is the right one, and 35% on the back foot. Preparing for the next blow, the back foot does not extend to the maximum, therefore diminishing the necessary time for the following application. At the same time that we apply the last elbow blow from up downwards, the foot bends to give extra strength in the lowering of the elbow, helped by the bending.

We have seen three applications of the Bulter master technique, on the arm, the leg and on the body. In all these applications some factors of importance stand out that I would like to mention so that they may be learnt well.

1. We move around the opponent.

2. All the blows are applied on the same element.

3. There are changes of positions with redistribution of weight.

4. Different blows are applied.

Ok, to all of this we must add that the performance in itself can be done in parts, without a hurry, but with maximum strength, and trying to cut the gap times between one application and the next; applying a strength to the striking of 80 to 100%, given the continuous movement in which something of strength is lost.
The Bulter technique recommends the alternating of the application of techniques. So, if we consider that an element has already received enough blows that have had effect, we can carry on to apply the technique on the nearest element or an element pertaining to the opponent which offers us some advantage because of its closeness, for its good position, for its importance, for its weakness, for something which suits us. It is also true that the available space has to be taken into account and the position of the opponent.
The aim of raising the left foot, in the application of elbow blow from up downwards on the opponent's spine, is to increase the strength of the blow by the creation of balance towards the right and then towards the left, a part where the application of the blow takes place.
I have been as explicit as possible on describing it, but assisting class is another thing, much better.
There is no book capable of competing with the explanations and demonstrations that can be done in class and, the most important thing, you cant ask me any questions reading the book.
But, who knows? I am waiting for you, I am ready and I await your questions. Maybe it's telepathy, I don't know, but someone, someday, will ask me questions without being with me and without knowing me. At first it will be complicated, but it is inevitable, we progress each second although we don't realize it, it causes no pain or bother, nor does the mobile phone ring announcing an incoming message, but it will happen. Let's see, someone rings the bell. Is it the door, or I am dreaming?
I am sorry, it wasn't the door, it was the microwave, I have the popcorn ready; I am sorry, it wasn't a message in a brain wave and neither was it a call from the dead through the switched off TV.
What a shame! I would like to know if in the other world there are libraries or if there is anyone interested in buying my books.
Next time, there is allways a next time or, La Prochen Foys, etc.

O. Oppressive Master Techniques

Oppressive Techniques are techniques that use a fast approach towards the opponent and once in this position butt, blow, kicks, head blow techniques are applied. That is, running towards the opponent, or applying large steps, we approach the attacker in record time.
The idea is to surprise the opponent, for which we have to imagine a train that passes without stopping in a train station.
Well, if you prefer, you can substitute the train with the bull, or a lorry, what does it matter, you have to understand the idea, the rest is smoke, coming from my pipe! The areas in which techniques are applied can be:
the chest, the abdomen, the feet and other parts which may interest us.

I distinguish two parts of performance:
A: The approach,
B: In movement the application of the chosen techniques.
Translated into Chinese it would be something like this:
The technique is called "he pass without knocking (but behind there are fallen)." Ok, a bit of my Chinese humor, Is it because I have seen many films? "The dragon hits with its tale, the monkey jumps, the eagle grabs etc". With all respect to the Chinese people and Chinese arts, this was when my grandmother was looking for a boyfriend and it always amuses me. But I understand that this was the way of thinking in those times. What I don't understand is that, after hundreds of years having passed, why are more adequate names not given to present times? But, what does it matter that the dragon turns around or that the technique is called roundhouse kick, despacho etc .
Ok, break's over. The aim of this technique is that of finishing with the attacker in record time, if necessary thrusting him, throwing him 2 to 3 meters. Go in without knocking and if you do, let it be the opponent who is the train station. Ok, I am going to say, pushes with the shoulder can be used, with the hands, with the palms, striking in straight movement or not, we will see later. Much speed, correct choice of the moment of the application, application of the adequate technique in agreement with the position of the attacker.
Also the calculation of strength which is applied in the impact, if the techniques applied don't have 100% effect, what techniques are to be applied. They are things that may happen or not, but the brain has to go over them during the training because in a real situation, you don't think, you act, simply act, you are putting into practice what you remember, adopted acts for each situation, they adapt to each situation. Each situation, each movement is different, unique.
Before beginning the attack, make a quick study of the terrain, especially the floor, there are slippery floors that make a fool of you and can give you a few scratches in different parts.

The application of the rapid movement and the application of the most suitable technique.

Movement to the left preparing techniques and strengths.

Application of the chosen technique in opposite direction to that described previously with foot change in the advance.

Explanatory photos of the applied technique using movement in the shape of "V".

Watch out for the change of position from left to right (looking at the photo)

Preparation and taking of preparatory position for the application of chosen technique.

Attention to the positions that the feet adopt depending on each change of position.

Application of the technique. Look at the movement and final position of the feet, of the shoulder and left arm which is the one that controls the rocking.

Direct applications of a single technique.

6. STYLE OF PERFORMANCE

It is without doubt one of the most important chapters. Starting with the agreement that not everything is aim and hit, questions must be asked and answers found. There are so many styles and types of Martial Arts, and each day a pupil creates his own style, a modern one including his ideas and excluding or maintaining and modifying the old techniques. It is normal and logical, humans do not come to a standstill, and it is natural to progress. Progresses are made beginning with the simple fact that a person gets bored and begins, for example, to solder screws transforming this simple act into an art, that later becomes recognized and valued. Another person who gets bored to death begins to mix rice with beans, runner beans and peas, later he gets the idea of coloring sand and making pictures of colours. Ok, well in Martial Arts, those who have practised it, not everybody, but some creative minds, have seen that the style that they have learnt can be improved and they create their own style. And I can tell you that TAUDANC is the fruition of many years of study, more than 26, of study and painful rehearsals of different Martial Arts. I will tell you that TAUDANC apart from its exclusive elements, uses a new mental technique, different to those which I have known in my life. It is very simple, but simple and clear things are part of TAUDANC. Of its philosophy, its style.
And it is this: Apply the techniques imagining that your target is not really where it is, but some 15-30 cms further back, more to the right, more to the left. If you do it, you will get to know the quintessence of TAUDANC. Even students of other styles have been surprised, when trying it, by the different style of performance, by the different form of application and by the sensation that it provokes and for the questions it leaves.
Some said : “but this changes EVERYTHING”.

There is another performance style and I refer to the performance of certain techniques in a very slow way, something between the isometric exercises and the Thai Chi style performance.

The isometric exercises or isometrics, which we will describe later, have also been described and shown in detail in the initiation level of the first book.

These techniques, practised slowly (speed between isometrics and Thai Chi), have many advantages and are part of TAUDANC with separate performance or using the intermediary speed of the two.

I am going to recommend that you begin with these types of exercises with the technique of The Open Arms, and continue with the direct techniques and other parts of techniques that best adapt to each one.

What we want to achieve with the practice of these exercises is:

- The control and correct measure of inhaling and exhaling.

- A good blood flow.

- Learning of the correct performance of all the movements and learnt techniques.

- To train the mind to maintain and distribute the necessary strength.

- Accustom the mind to the controlled slowness, to the reduced speed, trying to relax the mind during the process of performance.

- Accustom the body with the specific movements.

- Learn to apply that extra bit of strength in each final movement, marking the end of each blow, kick or movement.

All this amongst many other things that happen in a superior and much more complex and efficient performance, but we have to start with something and what I have described I consider to be sufficient for this level of preparation.

It is not only everything that I have written but also the involvement of the mind in each moment. Be aware of each action, feel each muscle contract or extend, feel the air in the lungs in the ears, let the mind assimilate all these details and others so that once the lesson has been learnt it transforms into a habit, in something indispensable, pleasurable in its performance.

The techniques of the photos which are presented next may be performed separately, having their actions and other corresponding characteristics for a correct performance, or they can be performed as a chain of techniques without gaps.

www.trafford.com
d1mart@yahoo.es
5.Técnicas Básicas
ARTE Y SALUD PARA TODOS
TAUBANC
DAN GIUGLEA

www.trafford.com
d1mart@yahoo.es
5.Técnicas Básicas
ARTE Y SALUD PARA TODOS
TAUBANC
DAN GIUGLEA

www.trafford.com
d1mart@yahoo.es
5.Técnicas Básicas
ARTE Y SALUD PARA TODOS
TAUBANC
DAN GIUGLEA

www.trafford.com
d1mart@yahoo.es
5.Técnicas Básicas
ARTE Y SALUD PARA TODOS
TAUBANC
DAN GIUGLEA

www.trafford.com
d1mart@yahoo.es
5.Técnicas Básicas
ARTE Y SALUD PARA TODOS
TAUBANC
DAN GIUGLEA

www.trafford.com
d1mart@yahoo.es
5.Técnicas Básicas
ARTE Y SALUD PARA TODOS
TAUBANC
DAN GIUGLEA

www.trafford.com
d1mart@yahoo.es
5.Técnicas Básicas
ARTE Y SALUD PARA TODOS
TAUBANC
DAN GIUGLEA

www.trafford.com
d1mart@yahoo.es
5.Técnicas Básicas
ARTE Y SALUD PARA TODOS
TAUBANC
DAN GIUGLEA

7. DIAGRAMS.

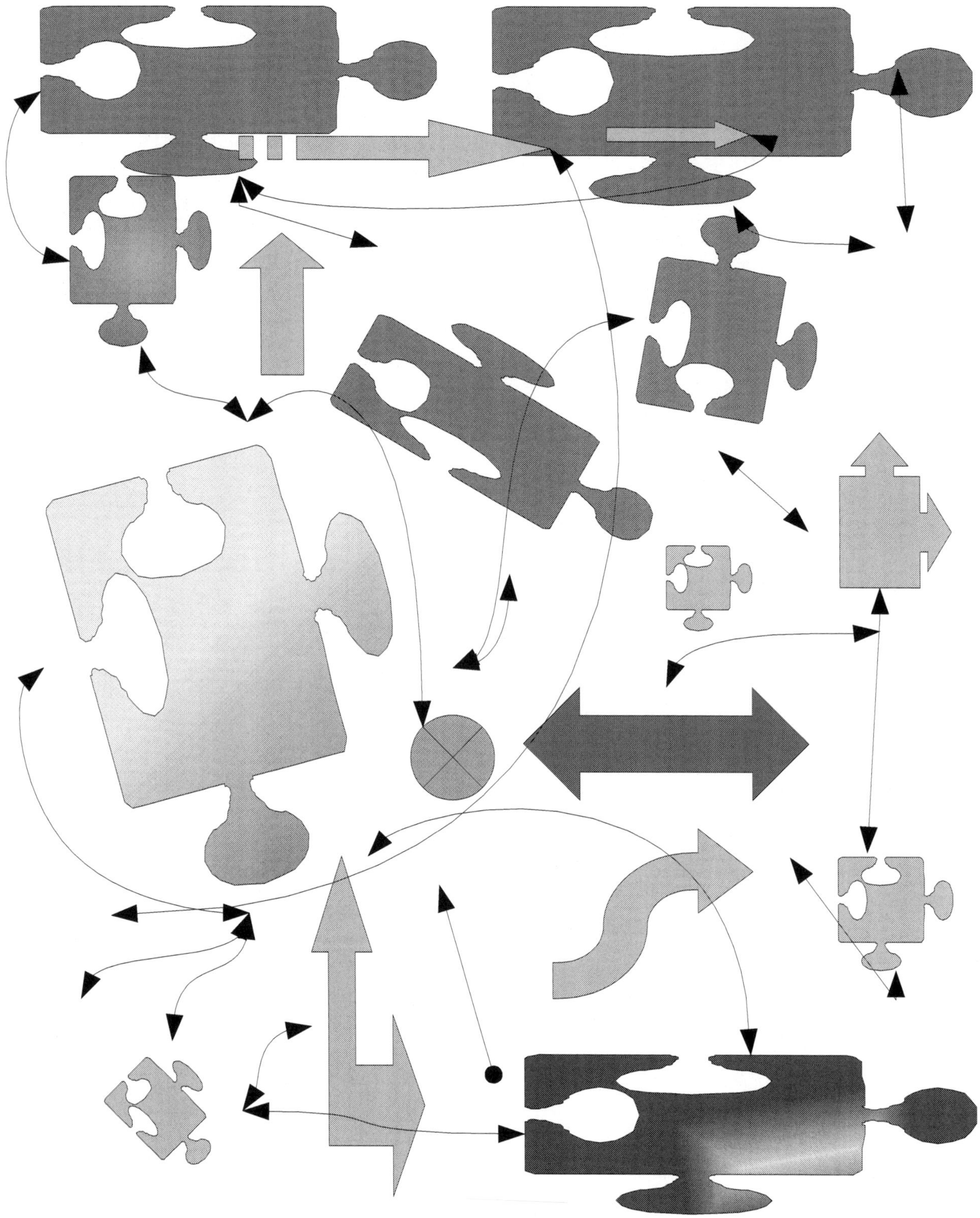

A DIAGRAM IS AN IMAGINARY FIGHT WITH ONE OR MORE ATTACKERS.

The measure of strength, inhaled, exhaled air, speed, technique, all depends on the imagination of each one.

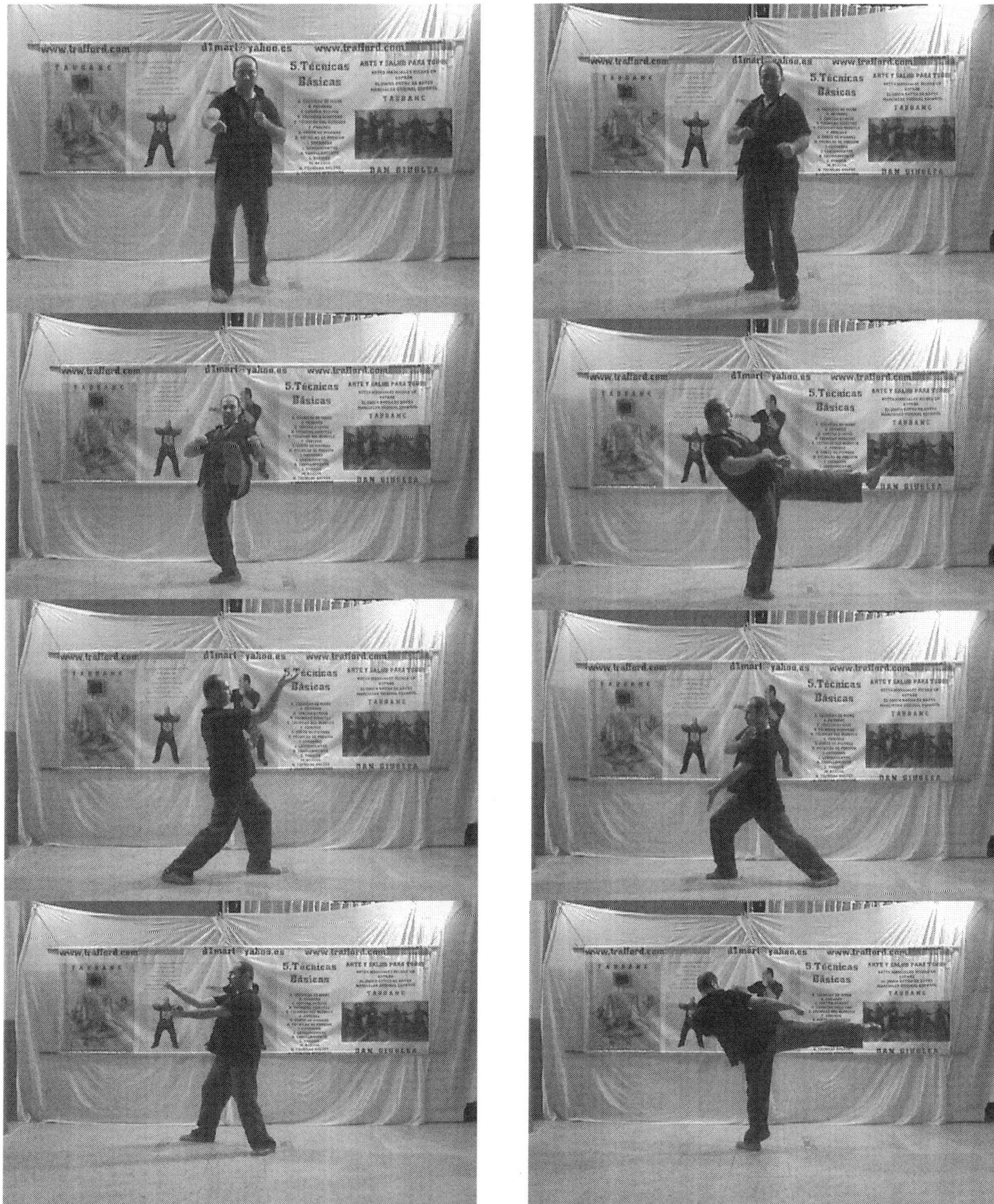

Ok, to help you a bit I will do other combinations.
They can be done, by looking, beginning from left to right or from top to bottom by columns, or in the order which you believe best.
I am using photos of performance of techniques with partners, but each student has to practise them alone, without help or instructions.

8. ADVANCED TRAINING

Made up of :

1. **Isometric exercises.**
2. **Contraction of the muscles with movement.**

The advanced training is a continuation of the usual training specific to TAUDANC shown and explained in the first book and is made up also of two parts.

a) Isometric exercises by techniques divided into isometrics for techniques of foot, kicks and hand techniques.

b) Exercises of contraction and relaxation of the muscles in movement, the composition of the two applied as one.

The isometric exercise applied to various techniques educates the body and its components to maintain the balance, to apply adequate breathing, to control the movements, the concentration and the focus. The aim of the contraction and controlled relaxation of the muscles, with or without movement, is to accustom the groups of muscles to said performances, contributing so to the good blood irrigation. The easy movement of contraction and relaxation is very useful in a confrontation, in defence and at times in attack, strengthening the point of impact. With the described practice elasticity is also achieved and good mobility of the necessary muscles in rapid defence or attack movements, giving a good general character to the body. The physical part of performance, also contributes to the formation and the education of the feet and the whole body in the correct application of each technique, particularly in different parts. An isometric exercise, applied to a performance of a side kick, can be described in the following way by parts of performance:

1. Take the position of performance of the side kick.
2. Raise the knee up to waist level and then bring the knee closer to the body.
3. Apply the corresponding breathing in such a way that we can hold this position for at least 20 seconds without moving.
4. Deploy the foot to the side in such a way that, very, very slowly looking for the perfect balance, together with the movement of the sole of the support foot to the back, we form the counter weight of the foot with our body to the back.
5. Hold in this position some 20 seconds to get the arms used to the corresponding position helping the body to maintain the balance.
6. Apply suitable breathing to give comfort, balance, as well as total control of the stability.
7. Perform the withdrawal and the deploy of the foot VERY slowly maintaining the distance from the floor and keeping total balance.

8. Apply inhaling and exhaling to the withdrawal and deploy.
9. Perform two actions one after another without a pause, slowly keeping the position still, but without tension, natural, without contractions.
10. Practise the exercise in a natural and relaxed way with performances of 2 to 3 parts one after another, respecting the seconds indicated above for the performance.

Other aims of the performance:
- To burn extra calories.
- Positive autosuggestion.
- To raise the spirit.
- To make the muscles agile, activation of blood irrigation.
- Diminishing of blood pressure.
- Reducing of muscular pains caused by stress.
- To develop muscular strength.
- Evaluation of the effort and performance.
- Gradual raising of the level of concentration and control.
- To recover agility lost through prolonged pauses.
- To obtain the psychological balance, which is learnt by controlling the muscular effort.
- To tone the muscular system, the lungs, the back, the stomach.

You have to be in good health condition.

STRETCHES

Stretches are very important and are an integral part of basic and advanced training. They are important for their easy performance and action on our bone and muscle structure which give the flexibility and the good functioning of the tendons and the extremities to which they are applied. They are able to reduce the muscular tension.
It is not essential to have a good physical shape, but it is essential to be in a good state of health, without serious injuries.
With respect to breathing, its worth mentioning that it is of vital importance to know how to breathe.
On inhaling and exhaling the lungs and the thoracic box act as bellows. The lung capacity is that of 5 litres of air, on taking a breath only half a litre of air is renewed, as in a deep breath 2 litres are breathed in, 2 litres are also breathed out.
Natural and correct breathing are very important in TAUDANC.
The muscles cover the body. Having elasticity they can contract and relax, with little differences depending on the muscle, their longitude, using them as necessary and generally to make movement easy.
It is known that the muscles obey the brain being transformed into active elements of the movement.
On stretching a muscle we find the reflex action of protection and withdrawal, for this reason it is not advisable to practise brusque stretches that can end up as unwanted contractions.

We could name the warming up or the training as the art of strengthening the body and endowing it with agility by physical exercises suitable to the use of TAUDANC. For a long time it has been demonstrated that gym was used in many places of the world as a religious and healing element having as its base the correct position of the body and the breathing.

Amongst these countries we number:

India, Greece, Egypt and China.

It is said that this practice was obligatory, since the year 600 BC. I personally find these methods, whether they are separate or combined, marvelous and efficient.

But in truth, we don't have to go so far back in time, the Japanese were doing it and they still do, in schools, in work places and there are many employees. So to be sincere, It wouldn't bother me, if before mass the priest asked us to do some exercises. It would be ridiculous? Why? Because we are used to everything that we have been shown or to what we have learnt by ourselves. What a mistake to have to live like my mother or my father lived. Because they are the closest to the child and of course they teach him the best they know but I think that we have to make the most of this so useful information, that in some aspects has to be filtered and analyzed and brought up to date.

I have already said it, the world and the man evolves each second.

If you don't believe me, you can try the hearts of Japanese fabrication with names of motorbikes or those of the pig that come from somewhere much closer, but we are going to leave it here.

What I tell you, before I finish writing a single word, will be called archaic by the mooners.

Who are the mooners ?

Well, those who already live on the moon, Chinese or Americans.

I have stopped.

Ok, to achieve good breathing read 5-10 pages of any book without stopping, with naturalness and if you are tired, you don't know how to breathe. Learn to read or breathe, or it is possible that you need to learn both things. Nobody is perfect, not even the mooners.

It may be that some things are repeated in this book, but this makes sense and it is done on purpose because,

" Repetition is the mother of learning ".

9. CONCENTRATION AND FOCUS

I will begin by saying that concentration, focus, and the body are interrelated resulting in a phase of study, decision and application. Concentration may be passive, giving the impression of being absent, but in reality, all the mental elements are joined together and are alert to supervise and control. Or it can be active, having as a main observation element the eyes and their movements of observation and control, leaving them the decision to act. This means that they actively follow the attacker's movements or the lack of them, in this case they allow the mind to make the right decision.

The mind may be directed in a natural, real and active way or it can already have formed a suitable behavior for each situation.

We are going to call this aspect "the educated mind".

When you have achieved an "educated mind", the behavior of the student is superior to that of the street fighter, or of another type, including people who have knowledge of martial arts.

The "educated mind" does not reflect any gesture of concentration, but in reality he has it all under control.

In the case of the directed mind, we make an interruption to make the decision and it makes us lose time, everything being analyzed by the mind in real time.

The difference consists in the aptitude of the educated mind to anticipate, therefore being more advanced in reacting.

It is so far ahead that we get to guess what the opponent is going to do, or try to do and the action will be even before the opponent begins to move. It is not about intuition, but about educating the mind, in such a way that you can sense and then take the necessary actions for the defence. A defence that at times is transformed into attack by the fact of acting before the opponent does.

Can an attack be qualified as a defence? I believe it can, it is only about anticipation and reaction which occurs before you are attacked, but the created situation demonstrates who the attacker is and who the defender is. It is just a question of time because the performance is brought forward.

To reflect too much has nothing to do with TAUDANC, too much thinking leads to confusion and the loss of reaction time, together with the creation of gap times; that is, moments in which the making of a decision takes too long. During training the mind learns to feel and direct the movements, breathing and focus.

The focus may be seen as an active, present and real concentration on a certain point or on the general picture of the enemy's situation.

Focus helps to channel the necessary strength in a determined direction, in the moment determined by the mind.

It may seem incredible, but if the mind is not controlled, it will control you.

Many times the mind races ahead and we find ourselves in the middle of an action without having thought about doing it, reflect.

Is it good or bad ?

It depends upon who has made the decision.

Unfortunately the mind is quicker in making decisions and, for the usual time to realize what or which is the decision you want to make, it needs planning, mentally visualizing the action which you are going to do, so we are able to distinguish and identify the author of the decision maker.

We, people, need to plan before acting and I believe that it is the only way to distinguish the author of our decisions.

Focus has almost always as a result an action, be it of defence, attack, study, situation analysis or simply to maintain the situation of alert. Concentration and focus are not always directed towards the opponent, they are used to harden the abdomen in a natural defence action, when we are being attacked in this area.

They are the directors of the breathing towards the attacked point and the distributors of the necessary energy for the defence.

Concentration can become so strong that you can receive blows to the abdomen or other parts of the body without feeling pain.

The phenomena is spontaneous and blocks the muscles, putting off the effect of pain to a later time, which may be an hour or until the end of the confrontation. I am sure that many of you have experienced this subconscious feeling generated by another impulse, the nervousness that has been the annihilator of pain.

Use the mind to direct, don't let yourself be directed!

It is necessary to learn concentration and focus to be able to control your own body, your movements and actions, and then to control your opponent.

Be aware that the mediation techniques of yoga are based on the concentration of a point or object "X", and on a thought, firm and continuous concentration and its effect is to suppress distractions.

So, I suggest that you think about how to stop thinking.

To be able to have the concentration active try to block the mental flow, when I do it, I feel on another dimension with a body of paper and without weight. Well, we are talking about provoking the interruption of the mental flow using a trained and prepared willpower.

THE POSITION, is an immobile position, the breathing slow and controlled, with the eyes open we choose an object or fixed point, next we close our eyes and try to define the object, it's position, it's color, it's size etc. We try to reduce the sensory activity until the distractions are wiped out. The important thing of this exercise is that once you have achieved this state, at this level you have two possibilities of application, choose the one you want:

1. Preparing yourself mentally by creating a suggestion by yourself.

2. Preparing yourself mentally done on the basis of suggestions from your sub consciousness, in this case your mind has stayed blank on its own wish and has left the initiative to the subconscious, your participation is a passive participation, of observation.

In both situations a projection of our ethereal body is experimented, an immersion into another world with the aim of knowing new barriers and mental potentialities.

These exercises usually last from 5 minutes to half an hour, the exercise ends when we take possession of ourselves returning to the world that we know, to the starting point, to the human condition.

Little by little, with practice we can get to have autonomy of movement in our immersion, in the LIGHT, in the darkness or on a Caribbean beach.

It is not about a hypnotic trance, but an imaginary journey that by its very existence gives us relaxation, concentration and the attentive observation of some details of our journey, as if we were going to have a holiday from ourselves.

If this is understood, the rest will come soon. RENOUNCEMENT is very important and has to be well understood, there are sacrifices that in real life can signify less worth, lack of decision etc. In the practice of TAUDANC, in many of the techniques, or in the performance of the concentration and focus or meditation, renouncement earns another meaning, of a tool used to reach another level of understanding by the renouncing of perception.

For example: the tick tock of a watch, at the time of mediation, or if it is about the practice of the techniques of renouncement by taking an attitude of attack or letting the opponent attack.

Only with the adoption of a low position by ourselves, we can make the opponent trip up in his advance and fall over. I recommend that you make a clear distinction between meditation, concentration and deep sleep. It should all be a controlled mental journey, nothing more.

As is well known, it all consists of positive and negative parts, so you have to be careful in which direction you travel.

Everything that has been said is of an initiation character and does not mean to submerge the student in unknown fields for which years of practice are needed and total self control without mistakes.

Neither are the techniques of meditation and concentration trying to distance you definitely from the illusions of this world, and nor do they give you marvelous powers, but the most important thing is what you believe that these practices are giving you, because,

BELIEF IS POWER.

The result depends on the effort of each one in particular.

It is nothing more than a meditative experience. Knowledge is directly related to the meditative experience, but also it is true that at a given time knowledge loses importance and the meditative experience gains form and desire.

10. SPECIAL TECHNIQUES

They consist of two parts:

1. Special techniques of mind training.
2. Special TAUDANC techniques and they refer to performance.

In the first part we begin by saying that to maintain a good state of mind it must be a daily task, even though we all try to do it in one way or another subconsciously. Doing it all consciously has another added value and in any case is important to test the options before beginning to do it. As not everything can be shown with a few words, I will tell you that once you have guessed the personal mental state, you can accelerate the practice of the performance of the themes that we propose ourselves to do with the mind.
Make the components of decision and performance, that later passes the orders to the performing parts, agile and give them greater fluidity and gentleness.

Some elements that influence the good use of TAUDANC:

- Level of skill.
- Correct solutions.
- Efficiency of the mental functions.
- Training of the same.
- Capability of logic and deduction.
- Capability of visualizing.
- Mental speed.
- Memory and good preparation.
- The dominant factor.
- Evaluation and action.
- Measuring of own capacities and those of opponent.
- Aims which we set ourselves.
- Good artistic capabilities.
- Intuition and elaboration.
- Determination.
- Intelligence to learn from personal mistakes and make the most of them.
- Simple and logical reasoning.
- Adaption.
- Understanding.
- To be what you want to be at the chosen time.

The scarce capacity of logic thinking, the lack of mental flexibility induces a spontaneous rejection of the newly learnt for which the mind has to be re-educated and directed to learn the immediate perception.

The strategy aimed at solving situations of any nature is:

- Constructive mind.
- Organizational capabilities.
- Quickness in perception.
- Determined skill.
- Easiness of correlations.
- Analytical capability that stimulates action.
- Good mental baggage.
- Reason in set terms.
- Capabilities of concentration and action.
- Not having mental targets.
- Do not think too much, act.
- Basic physical capabilities.
- Agile, versatile and set way of thinking.
- Practical capabilities of performance.
- Spatial perception.

Concentration, in a real defence situation, has another special character giving the Taudanc student the sensation of invincibility, cancelling of pain, increasing the reflexes and the speed in the performance, an incredible increase of strength in the applications of the techniques, making them light and at the same time hard.

It always has what is specific in mind without wanting to, it is like a state of euphoria with a great all powerful potential. Here human personality has a great deal to do with it and each component has to be questioned.

2. SPECIAL PERFORMANCE TECHNIQUES.

We are going to divide the special techniques into four, having therefore:

A. Special techniques performed with movements to the right or only left. This implies, the blocks, the kicks etc.

B. Special techniques performed with movements only to the back.

C. Special techniques performed only with movements to the front.

D. Special techniques of free style (straight kick to the side to the stomach) serves as an example. All the special techniques have a very important factor in common: the movement in various levels.

For example: If an attack, block, dodge etc. is started, the application takes place during and together with the chosen movement, that is, if we have chosen to apply the techniques in a straight line to the front, it means that in each technique that is to be applied a step to the front is given, five techniques-five steps and so on. The intention is to not leave space for the development of the opponent, obliging him to withdraw without the preparation of an adequate defence. It must be mentioned that in the application of the special techniques of free style the levels in which they are applied are very important, because the levels are those which impose the taking of suitable block, blow or counter attack positions for the performance of these techniques.

The levels of action or application are:

High, medium, low, the three corresponding to the three heights of the human body. We are going to focus a little on the performances at medium level, which should be understood as the space defined by the upper part, by the chest, and the lower part defined by the hip, and understanding that the medium level of the body should be seen not only face on but also from the sides and the back.
As it is a free style performance, in the area mentioned above, all types of techniques can be applied, from thrusts to blocks and continuing with any desired technique. For the performance of certain techniques facing the opponent a low position is adopted, determined by the flexing of the knees as much as necessary, leaving the base, combat position with the corresponding distance between the feet.
Example: Against an attack from the opponent with a blow towards our face or chest a combination of direct techniques can be performed. They can be made up of the performance at the same time as a block together with the punch towards the stomach and the flexion of the knees, so we have what we call action at middle level.
The three elements will be performed at the same time, independent of whether they are applied with step to the front, with withdrawal or without movement. In the performance of free techniques at the same level, but on side parts or on the back, the situation changes.
The position which has to be taken is always that of a low position with the knees flexed, but the movement will change which is now not to the front or to the back, but to the side.
The weight distribution changes and the distribution is different depending on the adopted position. The side movement, to the front or in withdrawal is being molded with the flexing of the knees in the same level and direction, in such a way, that the adopted position, assures sufficient stability and at the same time, offers the possibility of having more than one application, leaving space for the continuity, the application of following techniques.

SOME EXAMPLES OF SPECIAL TECHNIQUES

PhotoNº 1
Block at front level.

Photo Nº2
Preparation.
Photo Nº 3.
Withdrawal of left foot and the projection.

I have left this photo in the last position because it can be added to the techniques which are shown above. It can be applied as the first or the third technique. Said in another way, it can be the first or third photo between those of above or it can even occupy both positions, first and third performance.

Other Example

Block and neck grab followed by a strong rotation to the left, obliging the opponent to follow our movement.
Using the moving weight, with the left arm we direct the path which the opponent's head has to take, which is that of following the direction indicated by the movement of our body.
With two points to direct, we have the total control of the opponent's movement, who practically stops having his own movements once the turn is applied.

11. WARMING UP

The specific TAUDANC warm up is made up by the warming up of :
- Fingers and wrist, through stretching.
- Wrist.
- Stretching of the arms and elbows, right and left.
- Of the wrists to the inside.
- The waist and the back, practicing without partner the "foot cut".
- Back and legs.
- Of the neck by the sides in a 45 degree angle in slow motion.
- Of the knees inwards and outwards with complete rotation.
- Of the feet, each foot in turn, at 90 degrees with one foot below.
- Of the muscles by the jockey position, feet wide apart.
- Of the knee, by stretching in standing position.
- Of the leg, sitting position, at 90 degrees for each stretch and of the back with twist to the left.
- Of the foot with complete rotations, in sitting position.
- Of the legs, by stretching, sitting down.
- Of the hip with support on each foot in turn, standing position.
- The shoulders.
- The shoulders with hip twist, with the hands held high.
- The shoulders and contraction of the spine with hands high.
- Of the abdomen and the chest by stretching and raising the heels, the palms facing upwards.
- Isometric exercises under the door frame.
- Legs by front and side stretching.
- BREATHING, OTHER STRETCHES.
- CONTRACTION AND MUSCULAR RELAXATION, we will begin with the arms, followed by: the pectorals, abdomen, neck and legs.
- MEDITATAION AND RELAXATION during 3 minutes, sitting down.
- Gentle performances of techniques without partner.

SPECIAL WARM UP

- Of the legs by lifting them to the maximum and trying to touch the shoulder with the knee, the foot.
- Performance of side kick at middle level after slowly opening out the foot, it moves at vertical level up and downwards.
- Bend the body with the soles of the feet together, knees perfectly extended, without forcing.

Warming up helps us to keep ourselves in shape, because a body in shape is a body that can do daily tasks without getting tired and without being out of breath. We need to warm up to obtain flexibility, resistance and strength.
If the muscles are warm they will work more efficiently, be careful with everything, there are no spare parts.

1986

1986

1987

PHOTOS TAKEN IN A TIME AND COUNTRY WHERE
MARTIAL ARTS WERE PROHIBITED
BUT,
NOT FOR THE SPECIAL TROOPS OF THE
DEPARTMENT OF DEFENCE OF THE STATE.

**THE FIRST BOOK IN ENGLISH & SPANISH
PUBLICITY POSTER.**

13. MEDITATION

We are what we eat,

We are what we think,

We are what we dream,

We are what we imagine,

We are what we believe.

We are what we are, but I am tired of being something for so long and I need some meditation to clarify myself.

So, let's meditate!

Learn to feel good.

On finishing physical exercise, we sit down on the floor in a comfortable position, 3-5 minutes, with eyes closed and the mind blank. We pass from sitting position to position with the back on the floor, with the arms at shoulder level, in such a way that the body and the extremities make the shape of a cross.
The feet slightly apart by some 10 cms. We need nothing more than our energy, so without rings, watch, belt, without uncomfortable clothes or shoes.
Finding ourselves in this position, we pass to the cleansing of the mind, once free of any thought, we pass to visualizations provoked by ourselves, of an object or article that we like. Once the visualization is present try to describe the object mentally, its color, size, position etc. From here we are going to try to create visualizations of the practised techniques without adding to them their corresponding breathing during 10 minutes. We open the eyes, deep breath in, deep breath out, twice. One of the aims of meditation is the relaxation, a noticing of substantial changes at a physical and psychic level.
Meditation also means enjoying moments with ourselves, enjoying the silence, the solitude.
Breathing has to be natural, but deep, light and calm, trying to imagine that time has stopped and we can stay there infinitely, without a second passing.
All these exercises require practice and willpower, but I always find it like a space with no time in which I like to stay without getting old.
It is a real pleasure to live these moments, it is a marvelous therapy, a healthy one that fills you with energy.
Meditation also requires concentration, but I am sure that the student will find it very calming and pleasant.
The relaxing of one area of the body usually passes to the rest, depending which areas of the brain are used.
The obtaining of good results depends on:

- The understanding of the exercise.
- Perseverance.
- Capacity of self control.
- The nature of each person in particular.

Just like we have mentioned in the previous book, things have to be done that you are not used to doing, that you have never done, or you didn't even know existed. So we can number some examples:

- Count in a quiet voice from 1001 to 1009, have a break and repeat the counting raising the voice slightly, breathing normal and uncontrolled.
- Smile some 7-11 seconds, as wide as possible, while you are doing it breathe naturally.
- Open and close the jaw, as wide as possible, during 4-8 seconds.
- Close the eyes firmly for some seconds, with intervals of 3 seconds.
- Crease the forehead, raise the shoulders, contraction of the pectoral muscles. The mentioned exercises help relaxation with little energy and have to be done as many times as possible for days, weeks or months. They help in states of fatigue, exhaustion, illness, lack of sleep, depressive states, and headaches. Think that the parts of the body least used have to be toned up at least once a month so that the muscles recover their form and density. Finally, a stretch like the one that should be done on getting out of bed in the mornings, gives a general toning up of the body and drains it of negative energy.

Sleep is essential for health, it leaves the body rested and meditation can be done in a form of induced semi sleep, for which we will have semi controlled rest. Induction can be deep or light. We need to breathe air because it contains oxygen. The cells of the body need the oxygen to free the necessary energy for everything. Breathing can be molded, increased or decreased by the nose, throat, windpipe and lungs. From here a multitude of exercises can be done with variations of increase or detention. Breathing also moves your ribs and the diaphragm. The outward or inward movement can be easily noticed on taking deep breaths in or deep breaths out. As everything cannot be said in a book, nor in ten, I will limit myself to mention that the practisers of yoga, experts in reaching the total freeing of the mind and the soul, practise various spiritual exercises, the components being:

1. Abstentions,
2. Discipline,
3. Positive attitude,
4. Body positions that most help,
5. Null sensory activity,
6. Concentration and control of the above mentioned,
7. Meditation.

Revealing my method of practice and breathing control, I will repeat to you: when you have read ten pages of any book without stopping, without finishing out of breath, then you have reached the control of your breathing. Using another method, the desired rhythm of breathing can be achieved by breathing in, breathing out and holding the breath. The length can be the same or different, the important thing is to control these exercises.

Happiness is a good theme to use in our meditations.

There are many meditation techniques, but they can all be summed up in one phrase: stop of conscious perception, fixing of the thoughts as a contributive part to the technique or techniques.
Believer or not of any cult, it must be mentioned that in many religions, even in Catholicism, meditation techniques are practiced in which the priest says: "leave your mind free of all thoughts and talk to God," for example. For what we can see meditation and concentration exist from times we don't remember, but it is curious that there are some who say that many people exist who know nothing about the subject, and yet there are many who only with hearing the terms of the mediation techniques feel attracted, without knowing exactly how it is done. What a shame, we should all know about it from the day we are born: that is, we possess it, but we are not aware of this gift which strengthens, relaxes, cures and cheers us up.
Lucky us, that the body has its own defences and a percentage of self healing in case of illness which is usually between 15-18%.
In the majority of cases and when this happens we call it awake meditation.

14. TARGETS AND NERVE CENTERS

Also named as vital points.
A vital point is a sensitive part of the human body, connected or not to nerve centres that the student attacks in certain techniques with the intention of defend himself. For this it is necessary to know with exactitude the localization of said vital points and the sensitivity of each one. There exist many vital points; the main ones add up to 45, distributed around the body in categories and parts of the body.
Next we are going to show the most important ones which are the most attacked. Many of these points will receive attacks not only with the fist, but also with the finger, the knuckles, and the edge of the hand, given its small point of application provokes more pain.

HEAD

- Crown of the head.
- The space between the crown and forehead.
- Above and below the eyes.
- Eyes.
- Nose.
- Under the nose.
- Jaw.
- Behind the ears.
- Under the jawbone/jaw.

MIDDLE BODY/NECK

- Collar bone.
- Shoulder blade.
- Aorta.
- Humerus.
- Upper part of sternum.
- Solar plexus.
- Ribs.
- Inter rib spaces.
- Space between the shoulder blades.
- Base of spinal cord.
- Elbow joint.
- Back of the hand.

LOWER BODY

- Testicles.
- Knees.
- Ankle joint.
- Arm.
- Toes.
- Muscles.
- Ulna.

The nervous system is a network of communications that controls the body and its functioning, permitting us amongst other things: to think, to feel, to move, apart from all the interior processes.
The brains, the spinal cord, the spinal nerves, have a direct relation between themselves.
The brain is the control centre and at the same time receiver, taking charge of giving the adequate answers and putting them into practice. The reaction time also depends on it.
The spinal cord is a messenger service between the 62 nerves and the brain. It begins in the base of the brain and ends up a little further down from the middle of the back.
The nerves reach all the body. Amongst others, the informers of the brain are the senses of the eyes, the ears, speech, touch.
All of them send messages to the brain.
The blood circulation is also of great importance, pulmonary arteries that carry blood to the lungs, main artery of the heart, artery that supplies blood to the leg, pulmonary veins, vein of the lower part of the body. It must be taken into account that the main arteries transport the blood from the heart to the rest of the body.

IN THE NEXT BOOK

Master Techniques of weight.

Master Techniques of following the opponent.

Master Techniques in detail.
Other Master Techniques.
News about private schools of
TAUDANG.

GLOSSARY

A. Advanced training: Training followed from the basic warming up composed of various parts.

A. Adrenalin blow: Technique pertaining to the elastic hand techniques.

A. Attack: Technique used as defence in defence situations.

B. Bulter. Master Techniques that are applied on only one part of the body at a time.

B. Bonus: Extra material for the readers.

B. Butts: Bull pushing techniques.

C. Concentration and focus. Techniques of stimulation of the brain activities with the purpose of relaxation and knowledge.

C. Cut off air supply kick: Kick aimed to the solar plexus.

D. Diagrams: Application of free choice of fight techniques with one or more imaginary attackers.

E. "Ear Cut" Kick: Kick technique that applies a semicircular aim from down to upwards.

D. Displacement: Whole movement in application of techniques.

D. Dodge: Technique used to avoid contact with the opponent.

D. Direct Techniques: Technique composed of two movements performed as one sole movement.

E. Elastic Hand Technique: TAUDANC hand blow technique.

F. Foot cuts: Techniques aimed at cutting the opponent's feet with contact from the floor.

H. Hook: Foot technique that imitates the form of a hook.

H. Horn of the bull: Integrated part of the open arms technique.

H. Hand Master Techniques: Advanced techniques that uses only the arms and incorporated parts.

I. Immobilization in grab situations: Techniques that offer solutions to various grab situations.

I. Isometrics: Exercises destined to work certain groups of muscles, obtaining of the total control of the movements, balance.

J. Jump: Technique used in various techniques performances.

K. Kick Master Techniques: Techniques performed only with this and his parts.

L. Locks : Forms and union postions of the hands with various uses.

M. Master Techniques: Advanced TAUDANC techniques corresponding to level 1 of preparation and dificulty.

M. Master Combined techniques: Combination of tow or more techniques, performed with brakes between or, continuously.

O. Open Arms Techniques: Specific TAUDANC technique that is performed and defined by the simultaneous movement of the arms.

O. Opressive Techniques: Technique defined by the use of the fast approach to the opponent.

P. Projections, (Throws): Grab and throw techniques with the aim of folling down the opponent.

P. Pression: Techniques that applies pressure on vital points.

P. Patches: Technique of stucking on the opponent's body together with a lock or other techniques.

R. Real performances: Real performances, without manipulation of the photos by digital, photographical support or of other types.

R. Rolls: Mixed technique of following the path of the opponent's attack plus an added technique, grab, block.

R. Rotation: Movement used in various techniques as a component to the performed technique.

S. Self defence and Health: Integral part of TAUDANC, and the previously published book.

S. Spanish Martial Arts - TAUDANC: Martial arts inspired by the fight of the bull, the bull fighter, that of the English Bull-Terrier, that of the Flamenco Dance.

S. Special Blocks: Block techniques that require a certain performance and an advanced knowledge of the same.

S. Style of performance. Performance of techniques using the thoughts originating from TAUDANC.

S. Stop Kick: Foot technique applied aiming to stop the opponent's advance.

S. Surprise Kick: Special Kick performance,TAUDANC style.

S. Scissors: Kick technique imitating the movement of a scissor.

S. Special Techniques: Techniques corresponding to the level of preparation that this book shows.

T. The first "ear cut": Component part of the open arms technique.

T. The second "ear cut": Another technique of the open arms techniques.

T. Trick Techniques: Technique that use the distraction of the opponent with the aim to perform a totally different technique.

W. Warning: Aimed at those persons who can suffer damages without consulting with a doctor before beginning the physical or psychic practice.

W. Weapons: Instruments used with the purpose of training arms, wrists, other parts of the body.

INDEX

That"s All Folks, See you Soon, With Another Cartoon..................

Hoooooohoooo, Hooooohoooooooooo.....Hoooooooooooooo.........

DAN GIUGLEA
Member of the World Wide Net Of Writers in Spanish Language.

RED MUNDIAL DE ESCRITORES EN ESPAÑOL: R E M E S

- Principal
- Directorio de Escritores
- Cómo participar
- Ficha ejemplo
- Denuncias y Derechos
- Responsables de Remes
- Noticias para Miembros

A B C D E F G H I J K L M N Ñ O P Q R S T U V W X Y Z

- Giuglea, Dan
- 1964, Constanta, Rumania
- Callosa den Sarria, Alicante, España
- Oficial jefe de Radio Telecomunicaciones Internacionales, Director Comercial

Fundador y creador de las Artes Marciales Españolas

Acabo de publicar los 2 primeros libros en Español y Inglés,

TAUDANC Autodefensa y salud (Artes marciales Españolas)

TAUDANC Self defence and health, la siguiente estará publicada entre enero y febrero del 2008.

http://www.trafford.com/ 07-0365

http://www.trafford.com/ 07 - 2422

http://www.collectionscanada.ca/amicus/index-e.html

http://www.amazon.com

http://www.BookSurge

http://www.Abebooks.com

http://www.BarnesandNoble.com

- http://www.Booksense.com

RED MUNDIAL DE ESCRITORES EN ESPAÑOL: REMES

Principal
Directorio de Escritores
Cómo participar
Ficha ejemplo
Denuncias y Derechos
Responsables de Remes
Noticias para Miembros

A B C D E F G H I J K L M N Ñ O P Q R S T U V W X Y Z

Es importante leer las Noticias para Miembros Escritores Inscritos: 1344

028804 Visitantes

RED MUNDIAL DE ESCRITORES EN ESPAÑOL: REMES

http://www.redescritoresespa.com

Esta página Web-directorio nace con dos objetivos básicos y muy concretos:

- Ser un referente de consulta obligada sobre todos los escritores en lengua española (aunque su idioma vernáculo o habitual sea diverso) en cuanto a su bio-bibliografía general y específica, tanto para Revistas, como para Instituciones Culturales, Portales Literarios u otros escritores.
- Poner un importante grano de arena en la lucha contra el *habitual anonimato de la Red*, y, por ende, contra el frecuente fenómeno del *plagio literario*, que un instrumento tan universal y abierto (a la par que poco controlado) como Internet va propiciando cada vez con más asiduidad.

El éxito del proyecto –que no se oculta detrás de ningún secreto inenarrable, excepto de la transparencia- dependerá, sin duda, del deseo real y militante de todos los escritores a la hora de rellenar el formulario básico (http://www.redescritoresespa.com) y remitirlo a directorio@redescritoresespa.com , pero el propósito de los responsables de la idea es que pueda convertirse en lo más completo y universal posible.

Esperamos contar con la colaboración de la inmensa mayoría de los escritores en lengua española.

Gracias.

Issa Martínez Llongueras –México-

Luis E. Prieto Vázquez –España-

Responsables Generales de REMES

ISBN 142516913-9

9 781425 169138

1975352R00121

Printed in Great Britain
by Amazon.co.uk, Ltd.,
Marston Gate.